THE FOLK DRESS OF EUROPE

24 color plates
by Victor Ambrus

THE FOLK DRESS
OF EUROPE
James Snowden

MAYFLOWER BOOKS
NEW YORK

For my wife

All rights reserved under International and Pan American Copyright Convention.
Published in the United States by Mayflower Books, Inc., New York City 10022.
Originally published in England by Mills and Boon Ltd., London

Library of Congress Cataloging in Publication Data

Snowden, James.
    Folk dress of Europe.

    1. Costume – Europe.   2. Costume – Europe –
    History.   I. Title.
    GT720.S57   391'.024'094   79-1064

    ISBN 0-8317-3422-1

Manufactured in Great Britain
First American edition

Contents

Acknowledgments

My thanks are due once more to all those persons and institutions already acknowledged who helped in the compilation of my original bibliography, and of course, to the authors of the books listed in it, since without them this book could not have been attempted.

In addition, particular thanks are due to the following for kind assistance with the present work:

The Ethnographical Department of the National Museum, Prague,

The Ethnographical Department of the Moravian Museum, Brno,

Maria G. Veleva, Lily Ivanova and their colleagues at the State Ethnographical Museum and Institute, Sofia.

Zofia Jeż-Jarecka and Janina Skrzyńska of the National Ethnographical Museum, Warsaw,

Osterreichisches Museum für Volkskunde,

Ruth M. Anderson of the Hispanic Society of America,

Aagot Noss of Norsk Folkemuseum, Oslo,

Hans Deibel of Schlitz, Germany,

Ludvík Baran, Prague,

Georges Schmitt of Musée de l'Etat, Luxemburg,

Ioanna Papantoniou, of the Peloponnesian Folklore Foundation,

and to Jan Duyvetter of Nederlands Openlucht Museum, Arnhem both for bibliographical help and for information imparted in lectures which I have been privileged to attend. However, any mistakes of fact or opinion are solely my responsibility.

I owe special thanks also to my friends, Věra Kindlová, Rozalia Dmuchowska, Dieter Konradt and Karin Konradt-Dittmer, A. Laszlo, Roswita Obermann, Martine Ronssin, Françoise Sautes, Mary Jarvis and Ruth Bean for help in obtaining material, providing reminiscences and assistance with correspondence in their several languages.

Thanks are also due to Nottinghamshire County Library which supplied the travel books and other materials not in the possession of the author or otherwise acknowledged.

INTRODUCTION

The Nature of Folk Dress

When we speak of folk dress we mean the dress of the peasant communities and to a certain extent the non-fashionable dress of urban communities of Europe as it developed through the centuries. This development was at its height in the eighteenth and nineteenth centuries when conditions were most favourable, though strange to say, in certain instances, some of the greatest elaboration has taken place in the twentieth century; a last flowering as it were.

The widespread development of this kind of unfashionable but highly decorative dress gives the outside observer the impression, almost, of a national policy to adopt such apparel to represent each country. Whatever may be the function of folk dress in the modern commercial world—the antics attendant upon the *Miss World* competition leave one without adequate comment—this was certainly not the way in which it originated.

The development across the continent is, indeed, almost complete and does show a tendency to divide according to style, or degree of sophistication, along certain boundaries, but these divisions are really not between political but cultural entities. Long periods of foreign occupation or oppression have a marked effect on any culture and even brief campaigns can have an impact and, in fact, are fruitful of new styles both in the fashionable world and in the kind of society we are discussing. However, political boundaries in Europe have changed so often that in modern times popular cultures can only be made to coincide with new political identities by being exploited for patriotic purposes.

The rise of folk dress to its full development and subsequent decline was very swift, almost meteoric. The dress of the working people, apart from certain interesting local peculiarities, was for centuries rather uniform in colour and style, retaining much of the simplicity of medieval dress, especially outside the towns. Restrictive legislation caused it to evolve only slowly, then, when the legislation was lifted or ignored and elaboration became possible, local differences became more apparent.

The emergence of recognisable regional dress coincides with and is partly a product of the Romantic Age. This was the time when writers and artists first began to pay detailed attention to the life of the common people in the belief that it contained a lesson for civilization. Although the dress of the people was developing naturally and was not suddenly invented to suit the new observers, nevertheless their interest in it was to exert a great deal of influence, to motivate its development in the following century, to provide an audience for its display and eventually to invite participation from a wider section of the population outside the peasant classes. The self-consciousness aroused by observers, writers and painters created a feeling for 'our dress', a feeling that embedded itself in the organization and etiquette of village communities. Thus, a local dress was developed, including Sunday church-going dress, special clothes for weddings and feast-days and dress for dancing, fairs and the carnival.

In earlier times, village communities were isolated, not necessarily having good roads between them, but nevertheless having well-established services to provide their regular needs and the local means to produce and distribute their own goods. Within such self-sufficient communities there grew up an elaborate local culture and etiquette, partly based on religious observance, but always concerned with the survival of the community.

So, there were fixed methods of doing things, of arranging marriages and settling dowries, for instance. There were special roles for people of different age, sex and marital status. Ethical and moral standards were safeguarded, or at least, the rules for safeguarding them were maintained by rigid codes. Change, though inevitable, was gradual and although village life was exposed to the same influences and fashions as life elsewhere, they were delayed and the effect modified by local rather than international taste, if accepted at all. Of course, major incidents, like wars, which broke open the countryside, had the most powerful impact, but even enforced migration was not enough to destroy local traditions and there are many examples of alien minorities retaining their old customs and dress.

Because rural communities were self-sufficient in this way, their whole cultural life grew out of their daily activities and the yearly life cycle, centring round work, the preparation of food and clothing and the provision of entertainment for their hard-earned leisure time. The church, particularly the Catholic Church, was an important influence, since it provided the basic calendar of the year's activities, the fasts, the feast days and the weekly day of rest.

Out of this life cycle sprang a highly developed folk art which manifested itself in the making of utensils and pottery, the decoration of dwellings both within and without, the manufacture of textiles and the development of music and dance. We call it art, but of course there was originally no concept in the minds of the villagers of art for its own sake. The articles were for use and were decorated by the skill of the craftsman to make them more pleasing. The most decorative were for special occasions or for ceremonial purposes, but they were functional first and foremost. When the villagers wanted art, they bought popular prints and, later, photographs to hang on their walls, while the more discerning or well off might patronise the painter of the local scene.

An integral part of this life and culture was the dress of the people. It too could be divided into the functional and the ceremonial. It could advertise the regular or immediate occupation of the wearer, or his rank and marital status. As it was often regulated by quite strict usage which belonged to a particular area or parish, or geographical unit such as a mountain or valley, it could mark the wearer out as coming from that place. In some areas it was required of a person who moved from one community to another, to acquire the dress of the new community. This shows how powerful was the sense of local identity in these communities. The local dress played a key part in reinforcing this sense of identity through the intimate and personal involvement of the individual. We know from our own experience the power of fashion on the individual. Here we have, not the ephemeral fashion, but something of the same phenomenon, reinforced by the power of the community to condemn or approve any innovation.

Besides their everyday clothes, the people had their best clothes for church-going and the same, or frequently, other special wear for feast days and dancing. In addition there was usually a special dress or at least, a headdress for weddings. In these garments, on the making of which much care was lavished, we see the ceremonial aspect of folk dress. In the same way that household utensils might be decorated past the point where they were truly functional and became objects of prestige, the ceremonial dress was above all decorative. In its most extreme form, in prosperous communities it could be a display of family wealth and its elaboration was designed to convey the importance of the occasion on which it was worn and to underline the etiquette connected with it.

Because of this special function, there was not the connection between best and working clothes which we, unless we are very prosperous, are used to, where our best clothes when well worn are considered only fit for work. Since the nature of the two kinds of dress was so different, there was no question of such relegation. The ceremonial dress was reserved for its proper occasions and preserved accordingly.

On the other hand, there was a tendency, over a long period, for a style, as opposed to a garment, to promote itself, so that what was once everyday dress became at a later period a ceremonial dress, or alternatively, for an older style to be preserved only for certain special occasions, often occupations to which esteem attached.

These survivals were, one might say, rearguard actions against inevitable change. Folk dress, being part of a traditional way of life, is concerned, even consciously concerned to preserve itself against change, as opposed to fashionable dress, which seeks to introduce innovations and novelties, so that leaders of fashion can always be ahead of the herd. Of course, individuals in any community will have a taste for novelty and changes will be introduced from fashionable dress as its influence spreads into the provinces and from master to servant. Waists rise and fall and skirts alter their length. New fabrics are introduced to replace what was once hand made. Commercial products and accessories, combs, jewelry, lace, ribbons and other haberdashery are carried into the countryside by hawkers and pedlars to be bought with enthusiasm by the villagers. Gradually the basic styles become more elaborate and heavily trimmed.

There were economic as well as social reasons for rural communities to be conservative in their dress. Country people are naturally provident. They keep their wealth in goods and property rather than cash. A girl's trousseau might contain enough garments or cloth to last a lifetime. They deplore waste and expect their things to last. This was a particular necessity in former times. Even for a prosperous family, clothes would be expensive, especially the tailored garments of the men. Embroidered leather breeches, for example, can never have been cheap. Where the tailors were part of the local community or were regular visitors making their rounds, styles were apt to perpetuate themselves through the taste of the customer and the methods traditionally employed by the craftsman. Where the farmer went into the town to buy his clothes, he would not go to the tailor of high fashion and high prices, but to the man catering for his kind of customer, stocking reliable, old-fashioned materials, traditional in his skills and more modest in his charges.

In modern times, this very need for traditional skills and materials creates a difficulty for those wishing to continue to wear their folk dress.

In these days of mass production, the old situation is reversed. The traditional is now the most expensive and special materials and accessories become harder to obtain. Except at the highest levels, fashionable dress is far cheaper. Fortunately in this connection, folk dress is no longer the dress of a particular class, as it was originally. The class system itself has changed; rather rapidly in modern times, but with a gradual tendency over a long period.

Urbanization and the rise of a middle class brought with them burgher fashions, at first with the style of folk dress still informing them, and in fact often crystallizing into new elements of folk dress. However, the gradual refinement of manners tended to cause them to lose their vigour and variety. One can think of examples where the interest has become concentrated on the headdress alone, while the rest of the ensemble is plain, perhaps even black, owing to the importance attached to the observance of mourning. Alternatively it will be of an elaboration entirely inspired by urban fashion. I am thinking in the first instance of certain districts in the Netherlands. In some areas, the surviving dresses are splendidly individual, in others, sober to a degree, apart from their enterprising headdresses. In the second case, many of the Austrian dresses, surviving or revived, are of an urban character; moreover they have maintained that character since the beginning of the nineteenth century, for, with their silken materials and ruched trimmings they are almost pure 'Biedermeier' in style.

There have been times, including the present, when peasant styles have influenced fashionable dress, or when modish versions of actual garments have been adopted by fashionable society. This interest is usually only whimsical and plays no part in preserving the folk dress itself. The shepherdess styles of the eighteenth century had no connection with reality. However, there have been throughout our period examples of genuine patronage of folk dress which have made positive contributions to its development and survival.

By the last years of the nineteenth century, the social development in most countries towards urbanization, the growth of industry and the beginnings of universal education had almost destroyed the conditions in which folk dress could naturally thrive. It had been the mark of a particular class, but now the class system was breaking up. It does not take long for a tradition to disappear. When grandparents die and a new generation of children grow up outside it, the end has arrived. In some countries this was indeed the end; only in a few did the wearing of folk dress continue with any vigour. Fortunately, there were interested parties among the educated and noble classes anxious to prevent the old traditions from dying out completely, just as similar persons had been watching over and encouraging them throughout the century. But of course, it is patronising to expect people to keep to the habits of the class from which they are trying to break away. Why should they have their choice of clothes dictated? Why should they receive their fashions at second hand?

The factor which enabled the wearing of folk dress to revive and survive for a considerable time longer in the countries where this interest was taken was that the promoters of conservation took to wearing the dress themselves, so that it was no longer a mark of class, or necessarily of a way of life, yet remained a source of local pride. This was when the folklore and dance groups, the *Trachtenvereine* were started in Germany and Austria, the beginning of a movement which has spread, slightly spasmodically, between the wars and since to many other countries, sometimes with State support. Strict attention to authentic detail in the dress of different districts down to shoes and accessories, all based on the study of authentic sources, attempts to ensure that the styles are correctly preserved; it is an attempt to make time stand still.

Is it possible to discern a pattern in the distribution of the different styles of folk dress? Even the casual observer recognises a general similarity of style and decoration in the dress of neighbouring areas and even whole countries, a fact which unfortunately makes it easy to create a kind of all-purpose style without regard for authenticity or the finer details when costumes are needed for dancing, pageants or other fancy dress occasions. There does appear to be a common fund of inspiration in the decoration of both craft articles and dress. In painting, carving and embroidery there are certain almost universal decorative motifs, derived from the baroque style: hearts, tulips, trees of life, roses and human figures which may, or may not have symbolic meaning apart from obvious derivations from the Bible and legendary sources, but which certainly appeal to the taste of peasant craftsmen. Today, they still have validity as natural elements of decoration, probably because of their familiarity, even to people of sophisticated tastes. Yet, in spite of a superficial uniformity, one can discern a few basic styles, rarely quite separate or exclusive, but fundamental. They are most clearly discernible in women's dress, which has, through being 'dress-made' rather than tailored, retained more independence from current fashion until overtaken by ready-made clothing.

They represent, in fact, stages of development in the evolution of dress. In early times clothing was simple, of homespun cloth in natural colouring or dyed at home. In many countries there were strict laws governing the materials, styles and colours permitted for the dress of the common people in a largely feudal society. This tended to suppress change and a number of primitive elements were retained until quite a late date in certain places, to be incorporated into the folk dress as it developed in later times. The greatest degree of development has taken place in Western Europe, where the dress has come closest to urban styles. In contrast, in Eastern Europe it retains a more simple cut, which does not, however, preclude extreme elaboration of decorative detail.

The most widespread style in the west is the blouse or chemise and skirt, usually with bodice or corselet and/or jacket, together with scarves, shawls and other varied accessories. Sometimes the skirt is in the form of an open apron, which is a convenient way of putting on the garment. It is usual to wear several such skirts or aprons together, making the figure very bulky. The separate apron also has a decorative function. It concentrates the richest part of the ensemble at the front where it shows. In the same way, the front of the bodice may also be decorated.

The main style in the east is the long gown or shift of homespun cloth. The blouse of the style just discussed is actually a development from such a garment, retained as an undergarment. In the eastern style it has survived longer as outerwear, largely owing to Asian influence and Turkish rule. This style too, includes the apron as an important accessory. When the ensemble includes a long coat or overgarment, there may be a narrow apron in front, but in certain areas where short jackets are worn, a second apron may protect the rear also.

One encounters a rather singular style in places far apart in both eastern and western Europe which can perhaps be best described as a pinafore dress, hanging from shoulder straps or a small yoke, sometimes girded, often hanging loose. We see this in the *sarafan* of Russia, in Hallingdal in Norway, in two neighbouring localities in the Spanish Pyrennees and one in Switzerland to give a few widespread examples. It is evidently of ancient origin and serves as an example of the survival of a primitive style among more sophisticated later styles.

Men's dress also tends to divide into eastern and western styles. In the west, the wearing of folk dress by the men was discontinued in most countries before that of the women. It had usually grown nearer in style to fashionable dress, though somewhat behind. In the east, the styles, like those of the women, are simpler and more barbaric in cut but less restrained in decoration. The most splendid dresses, both for men and women are to be found where the two zones meet, notably in Hungary, Czechoslovakia and Poland.

Headdresses are also of great variety and include the crown-like hoods of old Russia, made up caps, coifs, chaplets and kerchiefs, either simply tied or bound and draped over supporting caps. One also encounters a wide variety of hats for both men and women. A separate study would be required to deal adequately with the derivation of headdresses and their relationship to one another but many derive from the French hoods and mob caps of the seventeenth and eighteenth centuries. Some customs are of ancient origin and have their parallel in the fashionable world, for instance the difference in headdress or hairstyle between women and girls or the married and unmarried. The fur cap, especially for men but also worn by women, is very widespread in European dress and some styles seem to be derivative, not only from ancient forms and earlier fashions, but perhaps from military styles also, as in the 'chair-cap' (German *Sesselmütze,* Czech *čepice stolice)* worn by young men throughout the Germanic lands and Bohemia, though in fact it is often far from clear in which direction a particular influence travels, and it may be that the folk dress influenced the uniform.

An accessory frequently encountered is the stout umbrella of strong cotton cloth, often red, the colour now thought to be usual, but also often green or black. These were popular throughout Europe. They were valued heirlooms. The red umbrella has been revived by the dance groups and costume societies as a typical accessory.

The sources for our study are numerous, though not readily available to English readers, and not all countries are equally well served. Since the sixteenth century there had been a fashion for producing albums depicting the variety of European dress, and with the development of Romanticism in art and literature, these became very popular, especially in countries on the route of the Grand Tour, but elsewhere also. They were, of course, popular with tourists and, more surprisingly, with the people themselves. It is even possible that they contributed to the growing uniformity of styles within a locality by providing examples. On the other hand people had, evidently, over a long period been conscious of themselves in pictorial terms, as we see from the wall paintings and votive pictures in the churches of central Europe—a fundamental source for the early development of folk dress. Fortunately a number of writers, particularly German writers, have used these as material for their studies.

From the beginning of the nineteenth century, important local artists began to identify themselves with the people they were painting and in their turn began to be recognized as 'our painter'. These were not primitive painters, but academic artists trained in Munich, Prague, Dusseldorf and Paris. The publication of prints still had a considerable market and in fact problems of dating and authenticity arise through the tendency to copy or adapt earlier examples. The case is happier when we know that the artist worked directly with his models and recorded the current scene, as many did, even into the twentieth century, for instance in what is now Czechoslovakia.

We can ourselves, appreciate what appealed to these artists. To the fashionable world, the peasant crafts, so evidently part of a long tradition, the pleasure of seeing the beautiful dresses so confidently worn, adding to the stature and dignity of the wearers and reflecting the stable nature of their lives, must always have seemed attractive to people whose own lives, for all their sophistication, were losing that stability. The appeal is still potent today. Perhaps, like the villagers, we relish ritual because it promises to keep anarchy at bay.

*   *   *

There is of course, another side to the coin. The Romantic Age in Europe soon became the Revolutionary Age and the people began to seek a political as well as a cultural identity. Central Europe had for centuries been organized under the Holy Roman Empire, and later much of it was under the Habsburg Empire; very few of the states of modern Europe had yet emerged. The movement towards independence, in some cases not won until 1918, was originated by intellectuals rather than the peasantry, but the commitment the intellectuals had made to the cultural heritage of their countries, to the language, literature and art, involved the peasantry and their folk arts in a political patriotism which they did not necessarily share and of which they were potential victims. The aspirations of a nation towards economic progress, education and improved living conditions were certain, sooner or later to threaten their way of life—and this has happened. You cannot detain people in sub-standard houses for the sake of their picturesque dresses and they do not transplant naturally to a new environment. This is why, as we see, the survival of folk dress and its often enthusiastic revival is in the form of festival dress, while the former traditions have become the subject of ethnographical study and the dresses the material of museum collections.

The interest in folk dress taken by the monarchy and ruling classes and later by their successors in the new republics, has varied in its effect and its effectiveness and also—and this has at times become sinister—in its motivation. Most of the royal interest stemmed from the German countries. The male dress of Austria and upper Bavaria, owes its very form and existence almost entirely to the adoption of the hunting dress of Styria and the Tyrol as a revived dress under royal patronage and in its turn adopted as official with appropriate variations for different districts by the *Trachtenvereine,* the costume societies. Moreover, the new royal families imported from Germany into other countries in the nineteenth century, took an enthusiasm for *national costume* with them. King Otto of Greece, from Bavaria, invented a national costume, based on Turkish styles, for his court. Queen Elizabeth of Romania, the German princess of Wied, married to the Hohenzollern King Carol I, used to require the entire court to dress in national costume when at the provincial capital of Sinaia. Her daughter-in-law, Queen Marie, who was English, also amassed a large collection which she loved to wear. This, if slightly comical, has its charm. The present government of Romania and that of most of the socialist countries takes a much more systematic interest in ethnographical study, preservation and display of local dress and encouragement of folk art, music and dance in general. Elsewhere there have been a few deviations when folk dress has been linked to nationalism of a more actively aggressive kind: the *National-sozialismus* which promoted the idea of the German master race. It is one thing to contemplate a picture of 'The Grand-Duchess of Luxembourg in national costume', or Queen Elizabeth of Romania in full rig; it is however, chilling to see pictures of Hitler with Eva Braun in Bavarian dress, or a group of *Oberlandler* wearing swastikas.

The pleasantest kind of patriotic folk art is that adhered to by emigré communities abroad to remind them of their homelands. The Poles, Ukrainians and Baltic peoples, exiled in western Europe, Britain, the United States and Canada, still run their dance groups with their re-created dresses. They may sometimes be less skilful, less professional than the visiting state dance companies from the countries of their birth, which they go eagerly to see, but their personal involvement must certainly be greater.

The Austro-Hungarian Empire

The countries making up the Habsburg Empire, together with the other German lands, could perhaps be regarded as the cradle of folk dress, in that more interest was taken in the dress, more artists depicted it and more was written about it from an early date than elsewhere.

The Empire brought together people of different races; German, Slav and Magyar, as well as the people of the Balkans, and this provides a point of divergence for the different styles from which it is convenient for us to start. We can leave Austria itself to be treated with the other German countries with which it has more affinity, and begin with the mainly non-Germanic countries central to the Empire, notably what are now Czechoslovakia and Hungary. The line of division between these two countries, though a political reality, is for our purposes slightly artificial. Czechoslovakia, within its modern borders, shows a division between the more developed styles of Western Europe and the simpler styles of the East, while between it and Hungary and the countries adjacent, the division is less sharp.

The reign of the Habsburgs did not go unimpeded in the southern part of the Empire and from the sixteenth century until 1739, Hungary was partly occupied by the Turks. For a century, Bratislava (Pozsony) was the capital, not Budapest. The Turkish influence on the dress of Southern Hungary, and indeed, throughout the Balkans, where the Turkish Empire spread, was very great. This was the second important influence on the simple native homespun dress. We have the pull towards western sophistication on the one hand, and the exotic influence of the east on the other. Perhaps the one accessory above all which became typical wear in the Empire was the Turkish style of boot for both men and women. It even spread into areas never occupied by the Turks.

16

Czechoslovakia

Czechoslovakia is a new state existing only since the First World War. It consists of the Czech lands of Bohemia and Moravia together with Slovakia, which previously was northern Hungary and is, therefore, rather different in character. The people are Slav, not Magyar and speak a language related to Czech.

The country provides a model for the rise of a national culture. Throughout the period of Germanization following the counter reformation in the early seventeenth century, the Czech peasantry were the guardians of the Czech language and the related culture. The growth of this, in the nineteenth century, enabled the new state to mature and emerge.

It was during this time that the dress of the people, especially in Bohemia was developing almost unobserved. The fashions, the accessories, the lace and embroidery; the tastes and skills learned by servants in the great houses, were gradually adopted into the peasant dress. By the mid-nineteenth century it had almost reached its height of richness and was ready to be exchanged for urban dress.

The areas where the peasant dress would survive longer could already be discerned. The painters of folk themes, of which there were so many, concentrated their attention most on these areas; notably Western Bohemia and Moravian Slovakia, that is, the borderland within Moravia, but all areas had their recording painters. Many writers also made their observations. For instance, the renowned writer Božena Němcová not only used her observations of village life in novels, but left descriptions in newspaper articles and correspondence.

The pioneers among these painters were the Mánes family, the greatest of whom was the founder of the Czech school, Josef Mánes, 1820–70. He made important studies of the dress of Moravian Slovakia and Slovakia, while his brother, Quido, painted in Western Bohemia. At a later date, Jaroslav Špillar, 1868–1917, was painting the scenes and people of the area around Postřekov, his adopted home in Western Bohemia, almost to the time of the decline of their dress.

The dress of the people of this area, called Chodsko, around Postřekov and Domažlice, is of interest and importance because it was the last to survive in Bohemia, yet contains ancient elements. It has also the most complete documentation. In its developed form, as modified during the nineteenth century, it relates in several details to other styles of West and South Bohemia. Here, as elsewhere, it appears to be the case that the most interesting developments in folk dress took place in borderlands. This is the border with Bavaria, and the Chods, so called from *choditi*, the verb, *to walk*, were in former times privileged as guardians of this mountainous area. It is, therefore, a conservative rather than a receptive spirit, in this case, which has made the dress interesting.

The two main regions of upper and lower Chodsko display important differences in the dress of the women, but are superficially similar. The main differences are the large collar of the upper (Postřekov) Chodsko blouse and a different style of jacket which retains a short pleated basque at the back. Formerly, when the whole style was higher waisted, the jacket, of blue cloth, had a long pleated basque. Young women wear black head-scarves knotted behind and embroidered on the corners which hang down. Near Domažlice, the fold across the crown is kept square by a large comb worn in the hair. Here, as elsewhere in peasant dress, black denotes youth, not age. The proper headdress for older women is a white shawl over the black one, sometimes tied with ends crossed under the chin and back on top, or with a separate chin cloth. The older style of headdress for matrons of Postřekov consisted of a bag-like cap, bound in position with a scarf at the front with a panel of black embroidery at the crown. These older styles are not seen in the revived festival dress. Pleated skirts, often red, are traditional but not exclusive features, with boldly striped and flowered aprons. Now a white patterned skirt is favoured for dancing.

The men, as almost always abandoned their dress as regular wear before the women. It consisted of a blue jacket and waistcoat with leather breeches—sometimes a long blue coat; not so very different from what was worn elsewhere. However, the older version had a long cream woollen coat of primitive cut. Fur caps or wide black hats were worn. This dress was already disappearing in the first years of the Republic for everyday wear. Today it may be seen during July at the lower Chodsko capital of Domažlice during festival time.

This festival, complete with dancing and bagpipes, is one of the three main festival gatherings held each summer in Czechoslovakia; one here in Bohemia, one in Moravian Slovakia at Strážnice and one in Slovakia at Vychodna. They are the result of a policy of encouraging the revival of the folk dress after the Second World War, a policy to which not only the revived dress owes its existence, but the surviving dress also, as supplies of necessary materials were made available at a time of great shortages. It was evidently thought to be a priority.

A close contemporary of both Božena Němcová and Josef Mánes, the composer, Bedřich Smetana, was also renowned for his interest in folk themes. His birthplace was Litomyšl, in Eastern Bohemia. The region was prosperous with many small towns and villages, and the prosperity of the people was reflected in a particularly elegant mode of dress. In Litomyšl, itself, the styles were urban, deriving from German and Austrian fashions—gold lace caps and all. The village styles, however, were also rich. The women's dress was notable for its variety of fine lace, bobbin lace, needlepoint and white embroidery. Here as always in Bohemia, the lace was invariably white, sometimes however, rinsed in blue water. The handkerchief-like headdress had to be arranged carefully on the head or prepared on a cap stand and it was held in place by a half hoop of metal, the decorative ends of which rested on the cheeks, to show in the final arrangement. Over this a plain long red scarf was tied or, for best, a fine white one the ends of which were exquisitely embroidered in white and lace trimmed. The elegance was in the details, rather than the silhouette, which was typically bulky; trimmings were exactly designed to fit, the bodice hooks exquisitely wrought, the stockings beautifully embroidered. The bodice, in the older style, was embroidered and laced with ribbons over a stiff busk or stomacher. Later it became plainer and was

4 Young man from Moravian Slovakia. Mid-twentieth century.

5 Slovakia. Man from Očova with a hairstyle widely worn in the nineteenth century. The subject died in 1945.

18

laced over a kerchief; in both cases over a blouse with ruffled neck. The
apron might be white with white embroidery or of a dark rich material.
The spenser-like jacket could be fur trimmed in winter. The men were
extremely smart, with a short jacket or waistcoat revealing an
embroidered belt. The high collar of the waistcoat was repeated on the
long coat of an almost conical shape. The hat was a very tall 'chair cap'
worn to the back, or a wide black hat with ribbons and a rosette.

Moravia provides a wide variety of styles, especially in Moravian
Slovakia. In this small area alone there are said to be twenty eight
variations. The dress was worn until recent times and a sort of generalized
everyday dress is still seen in the villages. Now the fine clothes are worn
for festivals, having been vigorously revived after the war. Indeed, this is
the area which responded most enthusiastically to the government's
scheme to restore the old customs; they had never been entirely lost.

One of the most prosperous farming areas of Moravia was Haná and it produced one of the richest and most complicated styles. Festival wear for older men included a long blue coat with a large fluted cape collar, worn like a cloak with the sleeves unused. With matching blue hat it was a garment of great dignity, not diminished by the fashion of wearing a large embroidered white handkerchief in the front opening of the trousers. But other areas vied in richness: in Klobouky near Brno, a great vertical frill of lace stood round the neck of the girls, passing in front of the face without an opening, and the men's hats sported on the top of the crown a high panache of flowers and tulle. This area surely must possess one of the most

8 Slovakia. Woman from Ždiar in the Tatra mountains in the festive dress worn before the Second World War.

9 Chod woman in cap by J. Spillar, 1901.

decorative styles to be found in Europe.

Hungarian influences are to be seen in the dress of Moravian Slovakia. For instance, on the men's sleeves which are cuffless and either wide at the wrist or narrowed to a 'leg of mutton' shape from a full top, and on the women's chemises, where the sleeves, tightly pleated at shoulder and elbow, are stiffened with paper and pulled out like a Chinese lantern. Similar sleeves are to be seen in the Highlands of Hungary. When we continue into Slovakia, these influences are reinforced. The country is narrow and the border never far away. In the vicinity of Očová and Detva in central Slovakia the former dress of the men was quite Hungarian. Even

21

braided hairstyles used to be favoured. The long sheepskin cloak could also be seen. A peculiarity was the short shirt which left the midriff bare.

Yet there is also great individuality of detail and decoration in the different localities. There is still, in the mountains, a vestige of the dress surviving and it can be seen on Sundays as well as at festivals. The everyday wear of the countrywomen, often of indigo-dyed 'blue-print' cloth is typical of an adapted simplified folk dress. The traditional festival dresses are magnificent and in some districts include headdresses of extreme complication. At Ždiar, in the High Tatras close to the Polish border, the styles, especially the men's, show an affinity with those across the border, where there is also pride in the traditional dress. Even the men in Ždiar sometimes appear in their thick white woollen trousers on Sundays. The women are famous for their skill in weaving and this is evident in their beautiful clothes.

10 West Bohemia. Man and woman from Litomyšl. Nineteenth century.

Hungary

11 Young married women from Kalosca. This style of dress is a twentieth century development, as is the art of wall-painting.

Since the tenth century when Arpád Khan brought his people from the East in victory to the Danubian plain, the Magyars have inhabited this area, absorbing other cultures yet maintaining their unique language. Their former area and population were halved in 1920, when they lost important territories to their neighbours; the effect was to make the nation even more homogeneous in character.

By nature and tradition, Hungary has always been an agricultural nation; only since the Second World War has the industrial revolution arrived. The feudal system in force before then meant that the large mass of the people were peasants. By contrast, more than half now live in cities and are employed in industry.

The native dress was still an essential part of Hungarian life before the war, adhered to by all classes, not only the peasantry. It also gave form and colour to the large number of military uniforms with their dolman jackets and braided breeches. It survives in places to this day and is encouraged by the present government, but current conditions are not favourable to its natural continuation. However, since 1953, the government has supported, with state funds, the Folk Art Council and the National Federation of Domestic Art and Craft Co-operatives with a view to giving the folk arts a living role in the culture and economy. These arts are most active in the areas where the dress is still worn and contribute through the textile crafts to its survival.

The richest and most colourful development was in the period between the two wars, some areas only reaching their height after the second war. However, the most typical garments of the Hungarian dress belong to an earlier stage of development.

The Hungarian dress was originally entirely the product of local materials, either made up at home or, in the case of the heavy outer garments, tailored and decorated by professional craftsmen. The narrow home-spun linen and hemp was made into chemises and skirts for the women and shirts and trousers for the men, all made with straight pieces to avoid waste. The trousers or *gatya* of the men were open at the bottom, while the shirts were usually without collars or cuffs; only in a few areas did a style with collar and cuffs develop. By the middle of the nineteenth century the abject poverty of the people had lessened owing to improvements in agriculture, and more prosperity brought the possibility of buying manufactured goods. This new factor began the change in form and colour which has continued ever since. Colour was introduced into the home spun cloth and embroidery decorated it. Rich manufactured fabrics were used for best. The garments worn became greater in number and the styles more distinctive. The movement away from simplicity was towards a European rather than an oriental style. Hairstyles, too, became momentarily fashionable; the 'Biedermeier' styles of the nineteenth century have survived almost to today.

The change was rather sudden and there is some disparity between the old styles and the new, which shows particularly in the men's fashions. The developed style is a cloth suit, but mixed styles have been worn since the beginning of the nineteenth century, when, for example, cloth jackets were worn with *gatya*. These mixtures and alternatives survive to some extent today. The *gatya* and wide-sleeved shirt, once developed as decorative garments, are promoted to festive wear and survive as such, even after the dress has become modernised. The tailored garments, imported from fashionable dress, were at first of blue cloth. Blue cloth

12 Northern Highlands, Hollókö. Married woman in everyday dress still worn up to the middle of the twentieth century.

24

breeches were popular with the well-to-do as an alternative to the *gatya* for best wear. Later, the blue colour was superseded by the highly fashionable black. Black neckerchiefs were a popular and smart accessory. Black was, and remains, a smart colour, associated with the best clothes of young people. Only with the passing of generations has it acquired an incidental connection with mourning. Originally in Hungary, mourning garb was white, as it still is in the region of Ormánság in the extreme south of the country.

The bought cotton cloth, used for the new shirts, chemises and *gatya*, was not tailored, however. The straight cut was retained, but the greater width in which the cloth was supplied was contained by pleats and gathers. The width of the sleeve and trouser legs became a fashion point which was developed and exaggerated.

Besides the old style of garment in linen and hemp, there were articles of outerwear made of sheepskin and wool frieze, in styles distinctive of Hungary. They were made by skilled craftsmen, organised in guilds and were much less amenable to adaptation, though each area had its distinctive characteristics. In the last century, the *suba*, a sheepskin cloak, was developed from primitive peasant wear to a garment of considerable elaboration and costliness; the mark of a prosperous man. Circular, or nearly so, and sometimes reaching the ground, the *suba* was cut with radial sections joined to a shoulder yoke. The long seams, which hung vertical when the garment was worn, were decorated with embroidery or appliqué on the skin side. Either the fleece or the skin could be worn outside. Women also wore the *suba*, but the female version was shorter.

Also of sheepskin were the jackets with sleeves called *ködmön*. Originally they were long and straight, but the later version is short and cut to fit. The embroidery of the narrow back panel is characteristic. Once worn by men and women, they are now worn mostly by older women.

The famous *szűr*, or coat of frieze, is surely the most characteristic garment in Hungarian male dress. It is cut in straight panels, in the old manner, and worn unfastened except for a strap across the chest to keep it in place. The arms are never put into the sleeves, so that it serves as a cloak. The turned back fronts continue the line of a great square collar which pulls over the head as a hood if required. The *szűr*, like the *suba* is decorated or embroidered. These traditional garments had their local versions, shorter or longer, wider or narrower, in all the regions of Hungary, each developing at different times.

Modern Hungary can be divided into three main geographical areas and it is convenient to refer to them in order to keep our bearings when discussing individual styles of dress. The country is divided in two by the river Danube, which flows north to south and on which stands Budapest, not far from the northern border. To the east of the Danube flows the Tisza, following a roughly parallel course across the Great Plain. To the north of the Great Plain, The Highlands form the Slovak border. To the west of the Danube the area is called Transdanubia. Here in the centre is Lake Balaton. Each area has important centres of surviving or recent folk dress and textile handicrafts.

In the Great Plain, near Debrecen, the chief town, lies an area called Hortobágy, renowned in the past for its mounted herdsmen in their blue homespun dress. Modern methods of stock-breeding have altered the picture, but each June there is a festival Sunday devoted to horse-herding, when the old dresses reappear. In the western part of the Plain, between the Tisza and the Danube, is the town of Kalosca. Here, and in the villages near, the folk dress has acquired a new appearance over the last fifty years with the development of multicoloured floral embroidery which covers the chemise, apron and headdress of the older women and even shoes. Young girls wear bright looped ribbons on their heads. The designs are the work of skilled women who draw directly on the light-coloured fabric. Other women practise the related skill of wall-painting, painting floral designs of a similar kind directly on the wall without prepared patterns. Also in this area, at Kiskunhalas, the world-famous Halas lace has been developed into a co-operative industry.

In the northern Highlands another craft, that of weaving, has been revived recently. This is the Palóc Region and its most beautiful village, Hollókö, is famous for its folk dress which is still worn on feast days. The most noticeable accessory is the headdress which consists of a decorated white coif with a kerchief folded narrowly with the fold on the forehead and the ends tied behind, so that the sides of the coif still show. Other villages wear a similar style, less sharply folded. Several short skirts and one or two dark aprons are worn. The puffed sleeve chemise is covered with a crossed shawl.

The most spectacular dress of the Highlands is that of the Matyó people in the vicinity of Mezökövesd. Strange to say, these people were never prosperous; they lived as hired hands, yet they preferred to put their earnings on their backs rather than to save them. The male attire represents the ultimate development of the decorated wide sleeve and trousers, though dark wool trousers or breeches are more often worn now.

13 and 15 Farmer and young woman from Hevés; from *Costumes de la Hongrie* by T. Valerio, 1855.

14 Peasants of Hadad, Transylvania; from *Sketches on the Danube*, 1838, by G. E. Hering, wearing untailored sheepskin mantels, while the woman wears a suba.

26

The sleeves are enormously wide and decorated with deep bands of coloured embroidery, or with white for a wedding. The women's dress is long and though wide at the hem, has graceful rather than bulky lines. The headdress is a kerchief, often supported by a wicker framework, but sometimes decorated with coloured pompons. The embroidery on the clothing is the most elaborate in Hungary.

In northern Transdanubia, at Kapuvár, the dress was also formerly long, but has become shorter in recent years. Here also, the headdress is high, consisting of a coif with long ends down behind, or a red kerchief, supported underneath. A white lacy embroidered kerchief may be worn over this, giving an elegant, almost aristocratic appearance. The dark, rich, bought materials of the dress, contrasting with fine white frills, add to this effect. Ordinarily a black silk apron is worn and coloured kerchiefs about neck and waist, but white aprons and kerchiefs are favoured for dancing.

The most splendid dresses surviving in Hungary are in the Sárköz region in the south of Transdanubia, near the Danube. Here a number of villages near Decs benefited most from the improvement of agriculture in the nineteenth century. For their dresses they began to use silks and brocades and their homespun fabrics became elaborately patterned. Moreover, they equipped themselves with more garments, wearing more at a time and preparing trousseaus of up to sixteen sets of clothing. Today, though declining, the dresses are splendid at festival time. The most noticeable feature is the wide spread of the numerous petticoats. The foundation for this is a gathered white linen skirt, many yards wide, with

16 *Left:* from the region of Pest. *Right:* on the banks of the River Tisza, by T. Valerio. The men are wearing gatya and szür coats. The one on the right has a black neck cloth.

white cotton petticoats and a coloured skirt with contrasting bands and a matching apron on the top. Over the bodice several heavily fringed shawls are worn, as many as four at once. A beaded collar and an embroidered coif add to the rich effect. Formerly boots were worn, but now, coloured knitted stockings with a raised pattern, and shoes, are favoured.

Until 1920, Transylvania, the neighbouring territory to the east, had belonged to Hungary for centuries, but it now belongs to Romania. Romanians (Wallachians) had always inhabited the country and after the end of Turkish rule the number increased. Resettlement in this century means that the Hungarians and other peoples remaining are now minorities, though they retain their languages, cultures and dress. We shall return to Transylvania therefore, when describing Romania.

18 Northern Highlands, Mátra region. The ceremonial dressing of the bride. Middle of the twentieth century.

28

Romania

Romania has been a separate nation for little more than 100 years, since the union of Moldavia and Wallachia, and until 1864, when the peasants were freed, was a feudal state. Her boundaries have never been constant for long, but within her present borders the people represent a fairly homogeneous nation of great antiquity, apparently descended from the ancient tribe of the Dacians. At the same time, there are separate

19 Girl from Trascău in Transylvania by Franz Jaschke, 1821. The dress remained almost unchanged to the twentieth century.

recognizable minorities: Hungarians, Germans and Bulgarians in Transylvania; Bulgarians, Macedonians, Turks, Tartars and the Russian Lipovani in the south-east, all contributing to the folk culture of the country. In the south, however, both in the minority communities and in the Romanian areas, the folk dress has all but disappeared. One can still see the separate influences in Transylvania.

To cope comfortably with descriptions referring to the different regions one needs a rough idea of the geographical, if not the administrative, arrangement of the country. The large area in the north-west is Transylvania, a plateau edged by the Carpathian mountains to the north and east and the Romanian Alps to the south. The east and south of the country form a great plain with the River Danube forming the southern boundary with Bulgaria. The river Olt flows south from Transylvania to the Danube and the area to the west of it is Oltenia while that to the east is Muntenia where Bucharest is situated. These two areas form the old province of Wallachia. Between Oltenia and Transylvania proper is the Banat. In the north east are those parts of the old province of Moldavia and the Bukovina which are not in the Soviet Union.

During the twentieth century Romania has kept and even developed many of its folk customs, especially the winter festivals in the north which are still celebrated with appropriate festivities, ritual and costumes. These are not for the benefit of the foreign tourist, though in the modern world they may be becoming self-conscious. Other occasions, especially weddings are the cause of much spinning, weaving, and embroidery in the preparation of the trousseau. This involves the whole village and sewing sessions, or 'bees', to which the menfolk are invited to provide music for dancing, are still part of village life in the north. In the towns, of course, apart from 'folk' entertainments, the customs have quite disappeared.

The folk dress itself has retained a remarkably consistent appearance over the centuries. Only in recent times have the textures, colours and decorations modified themselves with the arrival of cotton and artificial fibres, aniline dyes and machine woven fabrics. Formerly, everything was made locally, if not in the home, from hemp, linen, wool and silk cultivated in the south of the country, and sheep or fur skins. Much is still produced in this way, even though cotton or artificial fibres may be incorporated in the hand weaving. The availability of aniline dyes and bought brocades has not drastically altered the materials of the folk dress as in parts of Hungary. Some velvet has been introduced into the finest dresses but mostly the textures have been enriched, sometimes with metal threads, and the colours strengthened. Even today the main colour is white, the cut simple but ingenious and the decoration colourful and extensive but muted rather than gaudy.

The basic dress for women is the long white embroidered smock or short chemise and petticoat, over which other garments are worn but which remains more or less visible. Some areas favour a skirt, often open or wrapped over and capable of being draped, worn with or without an apron. Others wear the double apron, one at the back and one at the front, not usually matching and not necessarily the same length. The headdress is usually a long silk or cotton scarf, carefully draped, or a square kerchief, black or white and often printed or embroidered with flowers. There are also many individual headdresses including ones for special occasions. In Transylvania and Moldavia separate hoods, in a style said to go back to the Dacians, provide, or used to provide, protection for the head in winter.

30

20 Couple from Poieniţa Voinii in Haţeg Land, Transylvania. Early twentieth century.

Men wear tight or loose trousers according to locality. Very tight ones usually belong to gala dress rather than everyday wear. Black sheepskin caps and felt or straw hats are worn according to locality and season. Both sexes wear sheepskin waistcoats and coats as well as outer garments of thick wool frieze.

In the Banat, a prosperous agricultural area where even in feudal times the peasants had special privilieges, the dress of the women is both decorative and novel. Near Timișoara the double apron is worn, but the back one, called the *opreg,* is a short panel of richly woven or embroidered cloth from which fringes hang, the weft left short at the sides, but the warp threads very long down to the hem of the undergarment. The apron at the front is also richly decorated in a variety of individual styles. The sheepskin waistcoat is often embroidered over its entire surface, the sleeved long coat also, though not so heavily. The woollen frieze coat is plainer. The men here dress soberly and simply, by contrast. The long white shirt with white embroidered edge, high collar and cuffs is worn over wide trousers tucked into high black boots. Earlier, moccasins and leg straps were worn. The wide belt is decorated with coloured embroidery. The embroidery on the waistcoat, though extensive, is mostly black with a small amount of sombre colour. The cap is of black sheepskin.

Near Arad, not far away, the outline is different. The woman's dress in two parts; the blouse or chemise and white skirt are both embroidered, mainly in red. The embroidery of the skirt is concentrated at the waist, to replace a belt, and round the wide hem. A white lace-edged apron with many rows of woven patterns at the bottom, is worn over it. Formerly, the width of the skirt might be held out with wicker hoops. The head scarf may be decorated with a string of coins. Here the men's trousers are tight-fitting and embroidered over the thighs. The shirt, which does not hang over, is heavily embroidered in red while in contrast, the sheepskin cap, boots and waistcoat are black.

Near Hațeg in the south of Transylvania, we may also meet the fringed *opreg,* or alternatively a dark coloured, open, pleated skirt with a rather short apron in front. The chemise is often embroidered in narrow bands or lines of squares down the sleeves which are gathered below the elbow and full at the wrist, edged with embroidery. The footwear and hair styles are worth mentioning. The former consists of turned up leather moccasins bound onto the leg with straps over white socks. These were formerly universally worn in Romania and we shall meet them throughout the Balkans. The hair is plaited into rows of tiny plaits on each side which hang over the cheek and are caught up behind under a little embroidered cap. An alternative style, to be seen also nearer Cluj, is a plait at the front of the head as well as the back, the front one being draped over the right side of the face to plait into the one behind. There are several other interesting hairstyles in Transylvania.

The Cluj district of central Transylvania is extremely rich in styles, for here are concentrated not only Romanians but a number of ethnic minorities with their individual fashions. Perhaps the most interesting area, if one is to be chosen, is that of Bistrița and Năsăud, to the east of Cluj. The women's chemises nowadays are of fine cotton with delicate embroidery. The double woollen aprons are rather long and are decorated on the lower half. The waistcoat is embroidered velvet. In winter, warmth is provided by a long tasselled sheepskin coat. The men have tight

21 Woman from Bukovina. Beginning of twentieth century.

22 Young man's hat from the Bistrița-Năsăud region, as still worn today for ceremonial occasions.

Czechoslovakia. Young man from Bilovice and girl from Břeclav, Moravian Slovakia. 19th century
Tschechoslowakei. Mährisch Slowakei. Junger Mann aus Bilovice und Mädchen aus Břeclav. 19. Jahrhundert
Tchécoslovaquie. Moravie-Slovaquie. Jeune homme de Bilovice et jeune fille de Břeclav. XIXᵉ siècle

Hungary. Matyó bride and bridegroom
Ungarn. Braut und Brautigam in Matyótracht
Hongrie. Marié et mariée de Matyós

Romania. Couple from the Banat. 19th century
Rumanien. Paar aus dem Banat. 19. Jahrhundert
Roumanie. Couple du Banat. XIXe siècle

Bulgaria. Couple from the district of Trun, Western Bulgaria. Early 19th century
Bulgarien. Paar aus der Gegend von Trun, frühes 19. Jahrhundert
Bulgarie. Couple de la région de Tran, Bulgarie de l'ouest. Début du XIXe siècle

Yugoslavia. Youth and girl from the Skopje region. 1920
Jugoslawien. Bursch und Mädchen aus dem Gebiet von Skopje. 1920
Yougoslavie. Couple de la région de Skopje. 1920

Albania. Man and woman from Mirdita. Early 20th century

Albanien. Mann und Frau aus Mirdita. Früches 20. Jahrhundert

Albanie. Homme et femme de Mirdita. Début du XXᵉ siècle

Greece. Island of Chios
Griechenland. Paar von der Insel Khios
Grèce. Couple de l'Isle de Chio

Russia. Peasant from Voronezh and girl from Tula. 19th century
Rußland. Bauer aus Voronesch und Mädchen aus Tula. 19. Jahrhundert
Russie. Paysan de Voronej et jeune fille de Toula. XIXᵉ siècle

trousers and boots and rather long wide-sleeved shirts hanging over. The belt is very broad, of the kind worn throughout the Carpathians and adjacent mountains. The men's coats like the women's are covered with embroidery and coloured tassels. Decorated black hats, in some villages adorned by a great fan of peacock feathers (the birds are reared for the purpose) complete the ensemble.

The Bistriţa-Năsăud area has a minority of 'Saxons' of German descent, actually mostly from the Mosel valley and Luxembourg in the twelfth century, who still maintain their language and culture. Their dress is somewhat different from that of the Romanians, particularly the silhouette of the women. The shaped velvet bodices, the spreading skirts and wide aprons are characteristic, as is the headdress, either a bonnet-

23 Man and woman from the Bukovina, *c*. 1920.

shaped cap with strings under the chin or a cylindrical velvet headdress tied on top of the head with braid and decorated behind with jewelry and long pendant embroidered ribbons.

The Hungarian women of Trascău (Torockó in Hungarian) wear a dress just like that drawn by Jaschke in 1821, the crown or *párta* with broad ribbons hanging from it, the bodice embroidered with stripes. Although the stripes have become wider, the embroidered cuffs and shoulders of the chemise, the favourite white pleated skirt and green apron are unchanged. Now a folded square silk scarf may be tucked into the girdle and the girdle itself has a decorative clasp at the front.

To the east of the Cluj area, on the other side of the mountains, lie Moldavia and Bukovina, where the dress is still to be found in current use, not only at festival time. The Moldavian dress is rather simple and neat in effect, especially in the Bacău district where the short dark wrap-over skirt with thin woven stripes seems severe. In the Vrancea Mountains, there is more variation: the skirts are longer and the embroidery more extensive. At Putna, women used to wear a blouse of most ingenious cut, with very long sleeves sewn in a spiral and worn pushed up and twisted on the arm.

The men's attire is similar, without the decoration, to that of Bistriţa-Năsăud.

The dress of Suceava in Bukovina is particularly handsome and rather individual, though the main elements are the same as elsewhere in Romania. The men's narrow trousers are very long and worn wrinkled up to accommodate the length, with long or short boots. The thigh length shirt hangs over them and the sleeveless jacket comes somewhat below the waist. The women have a slender silhouette with a long tight wrap-over skirt, often with one corner draped up and tucked into the girdle of patterned braid. In winter, dark frieze coats or embroidered sheepskin coats edged with ferret fur are worn by both men and women.

The dress worn in Maramures, in the extreme north of Transylvania, is different from that of the rest of Romania, but closely related to styles in Hungary and eastern Slovakia. Near Baia Mare, white hemp or linen is worn in the summer and wool in winter. The men have very wide trousers, short shirts with wide sleeves and carry embroidered wallets or satchels on shoulder straps. The hats are small, of black felt, plain or decorated with patterned cloth and a feather, or of light straw, also with a thick feather. Fleecy sheepskin coats are worn in winter or slightly incongruous woollen jackets with horizontal stripes of more recent invention. The women's blouse top and petticoat are separate; the petticoat having an embroidered waistband instead of a belt. The top always has a square embroidered yoke, outlined and filled in with embroidery. The sleeves are gathered above the wrists with an embroidered frill below. The apron, normally now of manufactured cotton material, is chosen to match the main colour of the embroidery.

24 Young woman from Bilbov, northern Romania c. 1975.

Bulgaria

25 Young girl in the festive dress from Varna. End of the nineteenth century.

With Bulgaria we come properly into the Balkans, not just to the peninsula, but to the range of mountains which gives its name to the region. Here, in a comparatively small area, we can see examples of styles, in general outline found also in neighbouring countries. Yet, particular details mark the dress of each locality giving a truly national identity to the dress as a whole.

Bulgaria is an ancient kingdom, now a republic, which for 500 years was under Turkish rule and did not emerge again until 1878. The chief period of the development of folk dress was during the national revival when anti-Turkish resistance was at its height in the nineteenth century. The dress was a reflection of the cultural development with which the people compensated themselves and which also used the crafts and skills by which they made their living.

The dress itself is ancient and in its basic forms never developed much in the direction of the fashionable styles of western Europe. These were not, after all, natural models in this part of Europe where the Turkish influence was prevalent and where the basic style was mainly Slavic. Nevertheless, during the period of development each district acquired its own style, the differences being most observable in the dress of the women.

The country divides itself geographically into four main lateral bands. In the north, where the Danube forms the border, is the southern part of the Danube plain. Then there is the Balkan range of mountains together with the narrow range of the Sredna Gora where high plains, like that of Sofia, and valleys provide separate localities with natural divisions. Next, but only in the east is the Thracian Plain. The Rhodope Mountains extend along the southern border and in the extreme south-west the Pirin range runs for a short distance in the opposite direction, north to south. Thus the whole of western Bulgaria south of the Danube plain is mountainous, and it is these areas where the folk dress survived longest. In the plains, the dress began to decline almost at the time of independence, but the conservative nature of the people in the mountains allowed it to continue there, even to develop into the middle of the twentieth century. It is now, however, entirely gone from ordinary life and can only be seen at organised festivals and competitive rallies of which there are several in July and August.

The dress of the peasantry, our chief concern, was entirely home made, at least with regard to the woven and sewn textiles, and was also entirely the work of the women who prepared and decorated the garments for the whole family in addition to preparing food and working in the fields. Girls, of course, worked on their own trousseaux. There were, for the peasant classes at least, no professional tailors or embroiderers, nor guilds of craftsmen as in some neighbouring countries. Only the metallic

ornaments were made by skilled artisans in the towns and, of course, only the cheapest of these were afforded by the poorer people. Bulgarian society was both feudal and divided into mercantile and agricultural classes, all of whom had to supply commodities and provide services for the Turks, and who prospered more or less, according to what they provided. The Bulgarian dress, therefore, reflects these class divisions.

With these considerations in the background, the styles may be divided into three main ones for the women and two, with transitions between them, for the men. The women's dress may be of the double apron type such as one sees in Romania and the Ukraine, an essentially Slavic style, the *sukmán*, a closed, tunic-like garment of thick dark cloth for winter wear, and of linen in summer, usually with a low neck and with, or without sleeves, or the *saya*, a half-open gown, normally with sleeves. The last two are, in essence, Turkish styles. An apron may be worn with either of them. However, these are all over-garments. The basic, and originally the only garment, is the long white chemise of simple cut, made of home-spun and woven hemp, linen or cotton, the latter, though a local product, reserved for best.

Some of the main differences in the local styles are marked by the techniques used for the decoration of these chemises and overgarments. The area available for decoration depends, of course, on how much is on show; usually only the neck, breast, sleeves and hem of the chemise is embroidered, and if worn with a short-sleeved *sukmán*, only the lower part of the sleeve. Labour is not wasted on parts which are hidden, even behind an apron. It is not unknown for a *sukmán* to be provided with false sleeves, bodice front and hem to simulate a chemise, or for a hempen chemise to have cotton sleeves—indeed this is quite usual. On the other hand, infinite patience and skill are expended on decorating the chosen areas. The seams are also frequently made by, or marked by, embroidery stitches so that the construction of the garment is emphasized rather than hidden. Weaving techniques have been developed with a view to obtaining additional decorative effect. The finest chemises employ a method which produces a crêpe surface with a lengthwise direction which assists the hang of the garment. Often one or more pin stripes, usually red, is incorporated in the warp near the selvedge and provides additional subtle decoration to the seamed areas.

The embroidery styles are markedly regional in their techniques, colour schemes and motifs, providing strong clues to their place of origin. For instance, around Vidin, in the extreme north-west, the chemise is embroidered in subtle colours using sparsely the smallest, finely outlined motifs, to be found in Bulgaria. The chemise here is also notable for its special cut, with the neck shaped by fine smocked pleats. On the other hand, near Russé, also on the Danube but in the north-east, the embroidery is in dark and intense colours, heavily employed, containing motifs solidly worked in knots and rouleaux, and using many sequins. Though anthropomorphic and zoomorphic themes are not particularly common in Bulgarian embroidery, they are popular here, being used for repetitive borders of dancers with linked hands or cocks following one another, for instance, though always stylized, sometimes almost out of recognition. In central and western Bulgaria we find the embroidery styles which are regarded with most favour by the discerning. The Sofia district prefers geometrical motifs, usually red, well spaced yet combining with the background to make a larger shape. At Trun, in the west, near the

Yugoslav border, there is a great contrast between the hem and sleeves of the chemise. The former has long, linear, plant-like motifs in subtle colours, while the sleeves are heavily patterned, somewhat in the style of Sofia but with less background space between the motifs. Samokov and Stanké Dimitrov use integrated conventionalized floral and sunray motifs of great originality and beauty with a wide range of clear colours. Those of Samokov contain a preponderence of diagonal lines and those of Stanké Dimitrov forming rather square spirals. The patterns of Ihtiman, though less developed are related in character, especially the borders. Certain districts in the south east, like Haskovo and Harmanli, where the *saya* is worn, favour red and black striped materials for both male and female

27 Shepherd from Batak in the Rhodope mountains. End of the nineteenth century.

garments, as well as fabrics checked almost in the manner of tartans. In Thrace and the southern edge of the Sredna Gora there is more use of appliqué and the employment of small quantities of bought materials for trimmings, even tinsel braid sometimes. As in the illustration of the girl

28 Young woman from Goce Delčev in south western Bulgaria, wearing fine example of peasant jewelry.

from Stara Zagora, the lower part of a garment may be composed of vertical panels of different colours with a decoration of applied motifs. These contrast very much with the conservative styles of western Bulgaria around Sofia, Ihtiman and Kiustendil. Here the old styles developed the basic shapes with elaborate stitchery and the later ones tended to eliminate the surface decoration of the chemise in favour of knitted lace edgings in plain white, for which they eventually substituted machine made lace.

29 Young woman from Stara Zagora in the Thracian Plain. The appliqué decoration is typical and represents a more 'modern' development not followed in most parts of Bulgaria. However, the local dress disappeared earlier than in more conservative communities of western Bulgaria.

30 Young girl from Kiustendil in western Bulgaria in everyday dress, *c*. 1930.

In this region also, where the *sukmán* was universal, the cut of the garment was modified. Whereas the narrow width of the handwoven fabric normally required wedge-shaped godets from under the arm to the hem on each side, the production of warmer, fulled fabrics required a different layout. In this area the *sukmán* is normally increased in width at the sides from the waist down, giving a stiff skirted appearance. A typical decoration of the *sukmán* and also the dark outer garments of the men in the Sofia district consists of thick white lines with curling branches.

Besides the basic garments additional ones are put on either optionally according to the weather or required by etiquette according to status or occasion. Headdresses also reflect status and occasion; festive and bridal headdresses being usually very elaborate. The St. Lazarus day head-dresses of the girls from Sofia illustrate this very well. The headdresses of newly married women continue to be of great elaboration.

The dress of the men, as already mentioned, may be divided into two main styles. One, the older, is the 'white dress', in Bulgarian *belodreshnik*, which has narrow trousers of Slavic style and a top garment with strong Slavic influence such as might be found as far distant as Finland. The second, so-called 'Black dress', or *chernodreshnik* has trousers, baggy at the hips and tight from the knee, with a waist-length jacket—an oriental style. The colour, though black at its most fashionable in the dress of the towns is, in fact, varied. Garments are just as often of natural brown wool or of blue dyed material. In reality, the styles are not exclusive. The black style is seen at its most developed in the dress of prosperous artisans and in that of the higher classes, but in the conservative country areas of western Bulgaria the styles may be a compromise. Thus in the Sofia plain, for instance, one finds the narrow white lower garment with black upper garments, and in the Plain of Ihtiman one finds the cut of the white dress retained but made entirely of dark cloth.

Yugoslavia

Yugoslavia is another of the new states brought about by treaty after the First World War as the Kingdom of the Serbs, Croats and Slovenes. Only Serbia with Montenegro had been previously independent, since 1882 after the defeat of the Turks. The other territories came from the Austrian and the Turkish Empires. Though now one political entity, if with a certain degree of strain, the component areas retain their own traditions and folk customs.

In Serbia, particularly, there was no history of feudalism and most of the population worked the land as independent farmers. Consequently, in a village society, folk dress developed a strong tradition. In the former Turkish areas, especially in Bosnia, Turkish styles were influential. Moreover many of the people had found it convenient to become Muslim in order to obtain additional rights and their faith survived the transition to independence. In Slovenia and the former Austrian territories the styles relate more to Western Europe; the remaining territory of modern Austria is adjacent. In Croatia and Dalmatia, Italy provides an additional influence.

Folk dress was worn in most areas as normal everyday wear until after the Second World War, except in the north where it only remained as festival wear. By this time the large towns had developed their modern industrial character to some extent, and the dress was completely abandoned in many of them, apart perhaps from people coming to market.

Yugoslavian folk dress was entirely handmade from local materials, except for that of the gypsies who bought or traded for much of their clothing. Some of the finer Turkish styles, also involved manufactured textiles. Even cotton is grown in the Balkans, though in recent times cotton material is mostly imported. Men's clothes were also made at home.

Since the Second World War the picture has changed as the country's economic development has leapt ahead and modern facilities begin to come even to small villages. Apart from nondescript working dress, folk dress is now hardly worn, except in the south in parts of Macedonia and especially by the Albanian minority. There are one or two pockets of survival elsewhere, some of them surprisingly close to large towns.

On the other hand, the number of song and dance societies in Yugoslavia is very large and there are important festivals where the dresses can still be seen. There are also three national companies: Lada from Zagreb, Kolo from Belgrade and Tanec from Skopje which give professional performances.

The variety of women's dresses is very great, especially as there are differences not only between the old political divisions or the new component republics, but also between Christian and Muslim. If we leave aside Slovenia, where the central European bodice and cap are important components, the basic garment is the long chemise or separate blouse and

31 Albanian woman from Prisren in the Kosovo region of Yugoslavia, c. 1925.

42

petticoat with aprons, jacket and other accessories worn on top. For the men, except in the north where suits have long been fashionable, there are homespun shirts, either tucked in or worn as tunics, sleeveless jackets and a variety of trousers either wool or linen according to season. In some areas, for instance Prilep and Veles in Macedonia and in parts of Bosnia and Slavonia, men and especially small boys wear aprons as a decorative accessory.

The most elaborate attire for men and women is to be found in Southern Serbia and Macedonia, the latter now a separate republic within the nation. An example which has survived is that of Galičnik. The woman's white chemise, short sleeved and comparatively plain has a long sleeved jacket under it, frequently red with gold embroidered cuffs, and a waistcoat, also embroidered and braided in gold, over the top. One or two aprons are worn with a braid belt tied round the waist several times. These may be of striped or patterned material. Over all this a fringed shawl is draped, not about the shoulders but round the waist like another apron. There may on top of this also be the *pafte,* the metal waist clasp and coin and chain decoration typical of Macedonia and worn elsewhere in the Balkans also. The head scarf is tied to have long fringed ends hanging. At Prilep and Bitolj the women wind many yards of braid round their bodies from armhole to hip over their sleeveless jackets and also favour an elaborate hairstyle of many plaits found also in western Bulgaria. In other areas of Macedonia, as in Albania, the apron may be as stiff as a carpet

43

with thick fringe like a brush. Yet there are restrained styles, like those of Skopje, formerly Üsküb, basically of the same Turkish inspiration, but without the excessive draping of the midriff. Women of the muslim faith and a number of Christians also in Macedonia, the Kosmet and in Bosnia, often wear baggy trousers, (really a misnomer, as they are not divided into legs or only very short ones). Few women are veiled in recent times.

The dress of Montenegro, which always maintained a degree of independence of the Turks, has a specially barbaric appearance. It is the dress of mountain warriors, consisting of very baggy breeches, a double-breasted waistcoat, a knee-length tunic over which is a voluminous cummerbund and sometimes a sleeveless jacket which does not meet, though equipped on both sides with many buttons. Properly a formidable array of weapons should be worn, though the need for these is past. The

33 Dress of Risano on the Gulf of Cattaro, according to M. Bertrand de Moleville, 1804.

44

woman's dress of skirt, blouse and long or short embroidered coat may be simple or elaborate in cloth or trimming, according to rank or occasion. Both men and women wear pill box caps of red and black, those of the women having a scarf or veil hanging behind. These fashions were not peasant styles only, but universally worn, by royalty also, as the proper dress of the country, not as adopted 'national costume'.

Somewhat related fashions are seen in neighbouring Dalmatia and have survived in the Konavlji valley near to Dubrovnik where they may still be seen in the markets. They are less elaborate than the Montenegrin styles and nowadays rather uniform in black, white and red. Women wear large yellow tassels on the breast and either plain coloured aprons or, for formal wear, white or cream ones with a broad border at the bottom. While men and girls wear pillbox caps, the formal wear for older women is a winged

34 Nicholas I of Montenegro, ruled 1860–1918.

35 Macedonia. Women and children from Skopska Črnagora, near Skopje, about 1925. This was worn up to our times. Though the everyday wear is simpler, the enveloping headdress is retained.

starched cap, reminiscent of the Sisters of St. Vincent de Paul.

A characteristic of some of the old styles of Slavonia seems to be a quaint elaboration and formality with carefully parted and braided hairstyles. In Croatia, especially close to Zagreb there is still a surviving but rapidly declining tradition of folk dress. For instance the Zagorje area to the north of Zagreb, rich in tradition until twenty years ago, has lost much of its population to the industrial towns. However, in Lomnica to the south, the rather similar styles were still widely worn, at least by women, ten years ago and appear to survive. Here the dress, typical of the Zagreb area, is light in texture and unified in its colour scheme and decoration. The blouse, skirt and apron are all finely pleated and lace edged. The extensive embroidery, mainly red and arranged in bands, does not stifle the background. The whole ensemble is finely textured and elegant. The men's attire is also homespun, except for the bought cloth for the professionally tailored red waistcoat. The long trousers of modern shape are embroidered in a broad band down the outsides. A special accessory

36 Macedonia. Woman from Struga on the Yugoslav side of Lake Ochrid. Early twentieth century.

37 Couple from Lomnica, south of Zagreb. Contemporary, but fast disappearing.

46

is the tie, apparently the original *cravate* (Croat: *hrvat*).

Other areas in Dalmatia and Croatia have lost their traditions entirely, or rather, they are remembered, preserved in museums and revived by dance groups, but not continued in daily life. An acquaintance of the author whose childhood was spent in Split compares the scene of those days with that of today. At that time every region had its dress worn for everyday and also its wear for Sunday and festivals. The details of the dress revealed to the onlooker the station in life of the wearer. In a market town called Urlika, the girls of marriageable age would come down from the mountain villages on Sundays, their headdresses and foreheads decorated with coins and with banknotes attached to their aprons, thereby displaying their dowries. Outside the church after Mass, the villagers would join in dancing the kolo, a spontaneous activity, not a programmed entertainment. Now, not only have these traditions declined, but the working population has mostly left the area in search of work abroad.

Apart from the southern areas already mentioned, the region which preserves its old character best, both architecturally and in traditional dress is Bosnia with Hercegovina. Even large towns like Sarajevo maintain oriental bazaars and a good deal of dress of the muslim type is to be seen among the vendors. Small towns like Travnik are very typical of traditional Bosnia.

Albania

Albania, like the other countries of the Balkans, was subjected to 500 years of Turkish rule. Even after independence in 1912 the country enjoyed only brief freedom before coming under Italian domination when King Zog's alliance with Italy got out of hand. Real independence dates from the Second World War. Although, before the Turkish conquest Albania was in the mainstream of European commerce and civilization, by the end of the period the country was perhaps the most backward in Europe. The tribal organization, the only method by which the Turks could be defied and local affairs kept under native influence, had

38 *Far left and right:* Moslem women from Skodra (Scutari). Second left: Peasant woman from Malissor. Third left: Christian woman from Skodra. From Racinet, 1888.

developed into the rule of the vendetta and the blood feud to the extent that the economy was crippled and poverty universal among the peasantry, particularly in the north where the old law was strongest. Only the Turkish rulers, the local land-owning beys and the merchants were prosperous.

There were, therefore, two classes of people and two standards of dress. However, whereas in Western Europe the rich would wear the fashions of Paris, the same classes in the Balkans of the nineteenth century wore Turkish styles in rich materials. The peasant classes could only afford these as ceremonial dress, if prosperous. In Albania there was no such prosperity. Only in the twentieth century, even after the Second World War, were they able to buy such garments second hand, or to have their new clothes made from manufactured materials. Until then the dress of the Albanian peasant was homespun and locally produced. As we have already seen, styles in these circumstances are self-perpetuating, local traditions being all-important. A woman coming into the extended Albanian patriarchal family brought with her a trousseau to last a lifetime and was responsible for keeping her husband and children provided with clothes.

Within Albania there are two main divisions between north and south, divided by the Shkumbî river, based on tribal and language differences which also reflect themselves in the dress of the people. The northern people are called Gegs, the southern, Tosks.

In the north, the men of the Gegs wear woollen trousers, tight in the leg and jodhpur-like above, in the style seen in neighbouring countries. They are usually white decorated with black in summer, or dark in winter. With them a homespun linen, or more recently, a bought cambric shirt, a voluminous sash, a waistcoat and a jacket are worn, and on the feet, knitted socks and moccasins. Indoors brightly patterned oversocks replace the moccasins. The headdress is a white felt fez, sometimes bound round or covered with a scarf or turban. The old hair styles were barbaric, a favoured style leaving the hair in the centre of the head like a mane, the sides being shaved.

The women wear a gathered skirt over trousers with either a short chemise or a blouse which tucks in, or a long one, a fringed apron with coloured shawls above it, a low-cut waistcoat and a white homespun wool coat with sleeves decorated with embroidery. Headscarves or shawls are worn, tied high on the head, or in some districts a headdress decorated with coins. The coloured socks and footwear resemble those of the men. The styles of both men and women are like those of Yugoslavian Macedonia and Kosovo, and there are as many variations on the Albanian side of the border as on the other.

The old dress of the northern border city of Shkodër, (Scutari), was noticeably Turkish in character. The women wore extremely baggy trousers with the legs, in fact, not divided; the feet were put through cuffed holes at the corners of the bag-shaped garment. Catholic women would wear red, the Moslems perhaps other colours trimmed with gold braid. An embroidered chemise was tucked in and a sash or scarf bound round the waist. A sleeveless open coat with tight waist and full skirts, elaborately braided and embroidered was also part of the indoor dress. The head was covered with a large square or, for a married woman, a gauze veil. Out of doors the married women also used to wear a short red cloak with a large square collar which turned up over the top of the head. A

Moslem woman might have replaced the long sleeveless coat with a short tight one and the headdress would be a cap decorated with coins. She would have been veiled out of doors. In fact the Turkish influence on fashion in Shkodër was so strong that although the city was also the head of a Catholic see, the Christian women also covered their faces out of doors by drawing the points of their square scarves over them. As one might expect, the move towards western European dress started first in the large cities, and the native town dress such as this of Shkodër was no longer universal by the First World War. Remnants of it, often with eastern and western elements mixed, survived, until after the Second World War, though only among the older women.

In the south the men of the Tosks wear woollen breeches and leggings, light in summer, dark in winter, with a waistcoat and jacket, the jacket having openings at the armholes so that the sleeves need not be worn on the arms, a shirt with elbow length sleeves thus revealed, and a small cap. For ceremonial occasions only, a pleated kilt, the *fustanella*, is worn over the breeches. This is the dress which has also been adopted in mainland Greece. The women wear a long chemise over trousers with a short bodice and a long coat. Elsewhere in central Albania men wear baggy Turkish trousers and short dark jackets with large square collars and short sleeves.

Even after the Second World War, Albanian folk dress was widely worn, especially by women in all parts of the country and it could even be seen in the large cities (especially as they all had open markets selling country produce and native crafts including second-hand garments and new tailored garments of manufactured cloth such as corduroy). Since then, however, material and political progress has been so rapid that the picture is much changed. By 1965 the market in Tirana was abolished in favour of a palace of culture and by the early 1970s the only city with such a market was Elbasan. Recent five year plans have abolished religion, closed places of worship and put a stop to private ownership. Social welfare, education and economic programmes have all been speeded up and it is clear that the folk dress will soon become a casualty of progress, maintained no doubt through official programmes of culture.

39 Soldiers from southern Albania, from T. S. Hughes, *Travels in Greece and Albania*, 1820. The hairstyles with tufts remaining on a shaven head were worn by Albanian men up to the twentieth century.

Greece

40 Woman of Mantoudi. This illustration shows clearly the basic elements of Greek folk dress in a simple form. *c.* 1890.

With Greece and its islands we come to the southern extremity of Europe on the eastern side. Many of the elements of folk dress we have met in the Balkan peninsula are found crystallized in Byzantine splendour. Most of the Slavic ingredients have been left behind and the oriental flavour is now intense. Most of the splendour, in fact, is in the women's dress. The clothing of the men is basically rational and simple though there are certain eccentricities, some purposely introduced, for as already mentioned, national costume was promoted by King Otto and Queen Amalia.

As in the other countries in the peninsula the national borders have been rather fluid with the consequence that northern Greece contains certain minorities and refugees. The closing of borders in modern times has meant that nomadic tribes like the Vlachs and Sarakatsani have had to settle in one country or another and there are people of this kind who have now become Greek citizens but who keep their own traditions as far as possible.

The variety of dress, especially female dress, is bewildering. A regional distribution of styles is apparent, but within it there are so many variations of colour and decoration that it is perhaps better, at first, to discount them and establish the basic form of the dress. In central Greece the women's dress is basically a long chemise, often embroidered at the bottom and on the sleeves. This embroidery which is of great beauty and elaboration was normally worked at home. On modern versions of the folk dress it is much simplified; applied braids may even be used, as may be seen in post-card representations. There are overgarments of various kinds; short boleros, with or without sleeves, coat-dresses, sometimes two together, often of rich material. There is frequently also a coat of wool frieze, usually without sleeves and similar to those worn throughout the Balkans. Embroidery on these upper garments, often of gold, was the work of professional embroiderers. To complete the ensemble there are false fronts, aprons, sashes and added decoration worn over or under other items according to locality. The headdress is usually a scarf draped over a form of fez. Coin and chain jewelry is much used, both on the forehead and the chest, as well as belt buckles.

The men's styles may also be classified by region. In the north there are trousers of different patterns, in shapes seen elsewhere in the Balkans. In the main part of Greece, the *fustanella,* the full white skirt which originated in South Albania, is typical. On the islands the male nether garment is the *vraka. Vraki* are the very wide Turkish trousers with the fullness between the legs. Shirts, jackets and tunics of different kinds, usually rather simple, complete these outfits. The minorities and the people of the border areas have peculiarities of their own. The dress of Greek Macedonia and Thrace is closely related to that north of the border

51

52

41 Woman from Menidi. The ornamentation, though extreme, is quite typical for occasions when wealth needed to be shown.

42 Greek soldier. c. 1890.

in Yugoslavia and Bulgaria. Indeed, some of the people are resettled from one side or the other. The connection between Greek and Albanian dress is also evident.

The favoured national costume from about 1830 onwards was, or became, the town dress of the Peloponnese, worn also in Athens. The women's dress, known as the *Amalia,* consisted of a silk gown over a fine chemise with an embroidered front showing at the low neckline. Over this was a tight, gold embroidered, velvet jacket coming only to the waist, where it fastened. The flared sleeves of all three layers showed in tiers, one above the other. The headdress was a red fez, rather large and loose like a beret, with an extremely long tassel, the shank of which was a jewelled cord of gold braid. The dress of the men was that adopted first by the soldiers in the war of independence and was the basis of the uniform of the Palace Guard, the Evzones. Its original and richest form as worn at court was that of an Albanian chieftain. The *fustanella* was in its early long form. There were a varying number of sleeved and sleeveless embroidered jackets, the sleeves being actually worn with the arms inside them. A wide sash with a pouch, and embroidered leggings over tight white breeches, a red fez with a blue tassel or, alternatively, a draped turban, completed the outfit. As generally worn throughout central Greece, the *fustanella* became shorter, though less exaggerated than that of the Evzones, the jacket sleeves were not worn on the arm but hung behind like wings; the arms themselves in wide shirt sleeves emerging from an opening at the front of the shoulder. The leggings were not used in informal wear. The pompom on the turned up shoes soon increased in size.

The other versions of female dress in central Greece, i.e. in Attica and Boeotia, had their local variations but the styles were similar. The underdress was sleeveless, the sleeves being on the short bodice. A flared lower part was attached to the sleeves at the elbow, both parts being heavily embroidered, sometimes to match the deep embroidery at the bottom of the dress. This might have been gold, or mainly red and would have been the work of a professional embroiderer. Two sleeveless top-coats were worn, in wool or fine material according to the occasion, the upper one shorter than the lower and each with a wide border of red cloth. The lower edge was usually shaped into a tab near the front on each side so the two coats would have four such tabs. The hair, in two tight braids, incorporated heavy gold tassels hanging down the back. A light scarf was draped over a cap or fez. In its wedding or festive version, a great deal of gold or silver jewelry would be worn, across the forehead in rows of coins, on a deep collar, and on a front of chain net and coins. There would also be an elaborate belt buckle. In Phocis, by Mount Parnassus in the area near Amfissa, this style became simplified. The chemise was of unbleached silk, very fine with simple wide sleeves and a wide dark belt worn rather low. The white wool sleeveless jacket, cut low in front, accommodated the belt at the back only through slits on the hips. The jacket itself, too narrow to meet, was tied below the breasts with a black cord. A long narrow stiff red apron, embroidered in gold, was placed at the front and held in position with a black tasselled girdle, tied in the middle. The headdress preserved the fashion worn earlier of a white scarf decorated with many small white pompoms.

The women's dress on the islands, some of which have not belonged to Greece for long, was more varied and more bizarre. One of the styles of Crete, for example, has a white chemise over baggy trousers which show a

53

red, bustle-like, skirt, worn only behind and folded back to display a band of black silk, a white apron embroidered at the bottom in colour and a black sleeved jacket with shapes traced in gold embroidery. The red headscarf has a yellow fringe, draped to hang over the brow. In Chios, near the coast of Asia Minor, one of the styles has a sleeveless chemise and a heavily embroidered bodice, the long sleeves of which turn back to the elbow to make cuffs. There are two shawls or aprons in bright colours, hanging one on top of the other from the neckline or with the corners tucked into the armholes. The headdress is a specially draped small cap pinned on the side of the head.

The men's dress in the islands is all rather similar. *Vraki* of different degrees and length of fullness, in dark cloth, sometimes worn over white

43 and 44 Woman from Phocis. This dress is unusually simple and replaces an earlier style of greater elaboration.

54

45 Greek Islander from a drawing by Tristan Ellis, *c.* 1890.

ones to make them fuller, were the usual wear. In Crete, in earlier times, the central fullness would hang to ankle length behind. The slack was tucked into the belt when dancing. There were sleeveless and sleeved jackets, often with edges cut on the slope so that they were double breasted above yet did not meet at the waist. Extremely long sashes were worn which served as pockets. In Crete and some of the Dodecanese Islands long black boots were worn. Caps were varied in style. In Crete the men wore fringed scarves like those of the women, but black.

Unfortunately, hardly any of this richness survives today, except in revived and simplified form for rather generalized festive activities. Even while the national dress was being encouraged by the court, the general wearing of folk dress was in decline except in the rural areas. It should be remembered that western European fashions were not the natural fashions of Greek or Turkish urban society, except by adoption. This adoption was taking place throughout the nineteenth century. A visitor in the 1880s, Dr. Mahaffy, remarked upon this: 'One of the curious features of this century is the admiration for national costume among all the people who have lost it, and the low esteem for it among all those who still possess it'. By the 1930s there was very little left. On the islands the local dress lasted longer, in fact, until the spread of tourism.

The remote areas of Greece, particularly Epirus, were undeveloped until very recent times and the pastoral communities were some of the last places where local dress might be found. Even here the last twenty five years have transformed the picture. The change in the methods of sheep rearing, motorized transport replacing the herding on foot, the flight of the population to the towns and even abroad to countries like Germany in search of work, the advent of television—all these have ended the old life, wiping out hundreds of years of tradition, including the old traditional dress. While people, especially the older ones with no social pretensions, may still wear drab peasant clothes for work and everyday, their festive clothes have all gone—sold to the antique dealers and museums. The reconstructed dresses worn for tourist occasions are not of the same quality at all.

46 Lady from Ioannina. From T. S. Hughes, *Travel in Greece and Albania*, 1820. Ioannina was at the time part of Albania.

55

47 Dancers in the dress of the Island of Thassos. Twentieth century revival.

Russia

European Russia, the part of the USSR which we shall deal with here, comprises a number of republics grouped about the main ones of Great Russia, White Russia and the Ukraine. At different periods its western boundaries have varied. At present it contains the Baltic republics and what, between the two wars, was eastern Poland. The Ukraine has gained Ruthenia since the Second World War and part of Moldavia (Bessarabia) is also incorporated. A complication is that in the greater part of the area the folk dress had all but disappeared before the Russian Revolution, yet one needs to be able to refer to political or ethnic entities which are familiar. Russian Poland will not be dealt with here, therefore, except in so far as it is incorporated in the present USSR.

The territories mentioned, having had short periods of independence or attachments to other nations, may be expected to show signs of separate identity reflected in their culture but, in fact, the Ukraine, once the most important of the Russian territories, also maintains a vigorous character of its own. Moreover, the republics retain their own languages.

The year 1917 brought a new government to power and also saw the end of many traditions. Folk dress of a positive kind had already gone from a major part of Great Russia during the nineteenth century, as it had from other parts of Europe. In particular areas, however, it had survived with modified vigour, not entirely reduced to the universal working dress of the peasant. It continues now only in organized activities and on the stage. Even minority races like the Lapps, who retain their characteristic dress quite strongly in other countries, have taken on a Russian way of life. In that part of the Ukraine acquired at a later date and in the Moldavian Republic the folk tradition has survived longer, owing to the live tradition still there at the time.

The chief variations in the traditional dress of Great Russia were in that of the women. The men's attire was plainer in texture and more uniform in style. Decoration was not neglected, especially on the shirts, and summer breeches might be hand block printed, but the shirts, whether plain or embroidered had one universal pattern; high collared with the opening to one side.

The women's dress, though adhering to a few basic styles, provided more opportunities for adornment and for the use of rich material according to the degree of prosperity of the wearer. The dress was national in that it belonged to a different tradition from the fashions of western Europe. It was Peter the Great, as part of his plan to westernize Russia, who introduced, in fact, enforced at court the fashions of France to replace the old styles of the boyars. Later, under Catherine the Great, some slight flavour of the old national style was introduced as a reflection of the growth of Russian as opposed to international culture.

Meanwhile, the bourgeoisie, the merchant's wives and the peasants continued to wear the old Russian dress. As usual, when folk dress reaches a certain stage, local differences of style were developed, particularly in the shape of the headdress. The greatest discernible difference, however, is that of wealth. The silken garments of the prosperous are much more alike throughout Russia than the homespun dress of the peasantry. This maintained its local variations through being made locally by the wearers rather than being sewn by employees using bought materials.

The basic styles were of two kinds. In the north more exclusively, but also seen especially for richer garments in central Russia was the *sarafan*. This garment varied in construction but was basically a long flared tunic, usually fastened at the front and hanging from the shoulders on a small yoke or braces. Under it was a chemise which might be long and capable of being worn alone for work in the fields or in hot weather. On the other hand, since only the neck and arms showed under the *sarafan,* it was often the habit to wear a short blouse or even joined sleeves of superior material, sometimes patched together for economy. Such sleeves were often extra full or very long, when they would be worn pushed up on the arm. Over the *sarafan* one could wear a short flared, sleeved jacket, lined, padded or fur trimmed according to the occasion. These were in contrasting stuff, red being a favourite colour, or in material to match or tone with the *sarafan*. The headdresses worn with this style were remarkably rich, the most precious part of the whole attire. The *kokochniki* of the married women and the *povoiniki* of the young girls were made of cloth stiffened with cardboard: silk, velvet and damask—and at their finest were not only embroidered but ornamented with glass or jewels, especially pearls, not imported but the fresh water pearls of Russia's lakes and rivers. The *kokochnik* was made to pull down on the head to conceal the hair as was required for married women, but it also towered up or spread out or was padded to provide an area for decoration. Many *kokochniki* had pearl fringes on the forehead. Each district had its own style. The *povoinik* was smaller and allowed the hair to show. Even in the villages such jewelled headdresses would be used for weddings but they were mostly the property of merchants' wives in the towns. Needless to say, they were valuable heirlooms.

In the south the headdresses, equally or even more complicated in construction, and of strange shapes and component parts, pompoms, points, horns and hanging ribbons, were made of less precious materials but in brighter colours to accord with the more vigorous style of dress. In the centre and south while the appropriate classes might wear a silken *sarafan*, the main style was that of the *poneva*. This was a skirt worn over the chemise and usually with a long apron or pinafore, worn high like the front of a *sarafan*, sometimes with long sleeves. A loose straight sleeved tunic might also be worn, or a shawl or an open coat. Any or all of these garments might be patterned, either with patterns woven in the cloth or hand printed, or with woven panels incorporated in the construction, with embroidery or with appliquéd bands and patches of contrasting colour. Even the basic chemise could be heavily patterned by these means rather than discreetly embroidered. In winter heavy coats, capes and shawls were added and felt boots rather than the leather ones or the birch bark shoes, *lapki,* of milder seasons.

As time went on the styles tended to become simpler with the introduction of matching garments, often made of bought cloth under the influence of town dress, a tendency of peasant dress in western Europe,

48 and 49 The dress of Lower Lithuania in the nineteenth century. The pleated jacket was typical.

also. With this simplification, the headdresses lost much of their complication in favour of the headshawl or scarf worn alone.

The dress of the Ukraine is simpler or less sophisticated in its essential style but there are many variations, especially where it is transitional from that of Great Russia or from other neighbouring styles. The old basic garment over the chemise was the *plakhta,* a checked or tartan skirt with an apron covering the front gap. By the turn of the century a popular garment was the *corsetka*, a three-quarter length fitted sleeveless jacket fastening at the front, usually to one side. The headdress earlier consisted of a stiffened decorated cap with a veil, but later the veil was replaced by a manufactured headscarf. Aprons also began to be of bought printed calico rather than homespun and embroidered.

The blouses of the Ukraine and the shirts also were beautifully embroidered, floral patterns being more in favour than the geometrical or conventional animal and figure motifs of Great Russia. Coloured boots, especially red, were typical footwear.

The folk dress was well on its way to extinction by the end of the century or, at least, was becoming modified into that nondescript version of peasant dress which succeeds regional styles everywhere when handicrafts have fallen out of favour. However, the territories then in neighbouring countries, notably Trans-Carpathian Ruthenia continued the use of their dress well into the twentieth century. Between the wars

50 A south Russian woman. Nineteenth century.

Ruthenia was part of Czechoslovakia and a degree of pan-Slav national pride was encouraged; indeed an exhibition was mounted in Prague in 1924. The Huculy (Hutzuls), Lemki and other peoples of the area, with their related neighbours in Poland and the Ukraine, regarded themselves as separate even from one another. It will be observed how central the styles of this little corner of the Carpathians are in relation to those of the surrounding countries.

Within the boundaries of Great Russia and still remaining today in the RSFSR, were a number of racial minorities, in particular the Volga Finns. Of these the Mordvins or Mordovians are an interesting example who now occupy an autonomous republic, though as a minority and not confined to it. Their old dress was extremely colourful; simple but odd in cut, yet heavily decorated and with high barbaric looking headdresses. The women wore a basic chemise which was, however, adorned with boldly applied materials of all kinds: appliquéd cloth and coloured leather, beads and crochet work. A feature was the decoration by rolls of cloth or narrow tiers of coloured material up the back of the hips. A great many bead ornaments were worn, in particular a wide collar and long broad pendant. Headdresses were usually tall, one version being shaped like a closed bishop's mitre with a neck piece.

The Estonians are also a people of Finnish descent, but the aspect of their folk dress is rather different from that of the Volga Finns. Its elements were for the most part conventional, but a feature was a taste for massive jewelry of ancient design, notably a very large breast clasp. Headdresses were various, rather turban-like in some cases, sometimes plain headshawls and sometimes rather modest coronet-shaped ones, like those to be seen in Latvia. On the Estonian island of Muhu, the coronet was much larger, in the shape of a high open-topped mitre. On the island of Oesel the bridal headdress was in the form of a round, basket-shaped crown, while on Runo, it was a high, sharp cone.

Latvia kept its folk dress longest in Courland in the west, where it could still be seen at the beginning of the present century. It was given a most ancient and almost barbaric appearance by the medieval style of coronet

52 Woman from Ryazan. Late nineteenth century.

53 Trans-Carpathian Ukraine. Betrothed girl from Isa in festive dress in the first years of the twentieth century. At this time the region was not part of the USSR and local traditions were strong.

and the homespun linen or woollen mantle clasped on the shoulder with a large circular brooch.

The old dress of Lithuania, most characteristic of the northern part, consisted of a corset, skirt and apron with a voluminous headshawl, later replaced by bought scarves, and the *šimtakvaldis,* the long jacket with the pleated basque. However, this dress became extinct and when the national revival required a costume at the end of the nineteenth century, a form of dress from Suwalki was chosen which resembled that of Cracow in Poland. Men's dress was not revived except for folk dancing.

54 Woman from Archangel. This is a local variation in rich materials of the most prevalent style of dress in Great Russia. Nineteenth century.

55 Woman from Orel. End of the nineteenth century. Shows the apron with sleeves.

Poland

56 Festive dress of Łowicz. Contemporary.

For centuries the Polish peasantry was among the most severely oppressed in Europe. Attempts as early as the fourteenth century under Casimir the Great to alleviate their lot had had little effect against the intransigence of the noble landowners. It was not until 1760 that any serfs were freed at all when Zamoyski, the former Chancellor, released six of his villages in Mazowsze. The partition of Poland in the late eighteenth century lasting till the First World War, although politically disastrous, in many ways benefited the peasants by reducing the power of the landowners. Even the successive uprisings in the nineteenth century were ultimately to their advantage as politicians were discredited and dissidents fled deprived of their land. Moreover, the new imperial powers reformed the land laws. Both Austria and Prussia abolished serfdom and in the Russian Kingdom of Poland it was abolished by the Polish insurrectionary government at the time of the last uprising of 1863. Thereafter there were no serfs in Poland. Though holdings were individually rather small, the peasant farmers made themselves relatively prosperous by concentrating on stock rather than crops. They also, as the only stable section of society, became the centre of a romantic national movement. Austrian Poland, (Galicia) centred on Cracow, had considerable autonomy of government and independence for its social and cultural institutions. The Kingdom of Poland, centred on Warsaw, had no political independence under Russia above the level of parish councils, but was allowed Polish newspapers and a Polish language theatre. Consequently there were still the means of expressing such a movement, even though Prussian Poland was entirely Germanized. As in other countries, though somewhat later, the movement promoted ethnographical study which came to fruition at the beginning of the twentieth century when the first ethnographical museums were founded.

Polish folk dress had until a late period, therefore, been rather simple and undeveloped, based on homespun garments of linen, hemp and wool, with skins and fur added in winter. Much of the distinctive regionalized dress which developed in the nineteenth century relied first on dyed materials as opposed to naturally coloured fabrics, so that blue, brown or black cloths began to appear and, eventually, bought materials. So, except in the mountains, the area of Austrian Southern Poland soon lost its tradition of home spinning and weaving, as did Prussian Poland. Russian Central Poland, in particular the Mazowsze region (Mazovia), remained the area on which the folk dress relied on home spun and woven fabrics and this tradition is reflected in the styles surviving, or revived, today.

The Mazowsze styles, especially those of Łowicz and Kurpie region, have been made familiar all over the world by the famous Mazowsze Dance Company. There are, however, besides Łowicz, a number of areas circling the city of Łódź which together present an interesting picture of

the Mazowsze dress. These are the districts of Opoczno and Piotrków with the related styles in the adjacent regions of Sieradz. Adjacent to Mazowsze on the south east is northern Małopolska (Lesser Poland). Here too, the style is related and round Kielce, for instance, we find styles transitional between those of Mazowsze, and those of Cracow to the south.

The Mazowsze style, with local differences, depends for its effect on the use of boldly striped and sometimes checked garments, worn, as it were, in layers. The striped skirt will have a shorter, gathered striped apron over it and, for outdoor wear, a striped cape (shoulder apron) or larger striped shawl. At Łowicz, where all the domestic arts became very fully developed and where the interior decoration of houses, elaborate paper cutting and other crafts are still famous, the dress also became more decorative. The patterns became bolder until, in the latest development, wide bands of large flowers on a black background decorate the edge of each garment. The dress of the men of Łowicz also uses striped cloth, especially for the breeches, but, whereas a white coat of straight cut was worn for weddings and festive occasions at an earlier period, the coat is now always black.

The man's coat worn in Poland, called *sukmana,* is encountered in different types and colours according to period and degree of development. The earliest were the simplest, of straight or angular cut in natural wool or linen, sometimes with coloured edges. Coats of different materials or special styles often have their own names in different localities. In the Swiętokrzyski region near Kielce the *sukmana* became brown with red embroidery and blue facings but did not develop its cut, apart from the enlargement of the left lapel, a style seen also in the blue coats of Sieradz. It is in the south of Małopolska, near Cracow that we see the most development.

Before leaving the district of Kielce one ought to remark on the headdress of the bride. Polish bridal headdresses are in general highly elaborate and decorative, though less so, strangely in the south. This one, however, is very unusual consisting of a tall crown made of coloured ribbons twisted into spires like cones inserted into one another.

To the north west of Warsaw is the Kurpie region, an area from which the dress is also familiar from the performances of the Mazowsze Dance Company. The region vies with Łowicz in its traditions of folk culture. There are two areas, north and south of the Narew river: Puszcza Zielona (Green Forest) and Puszcza Biała (White Forest) with somewhat different styles of dress—especially that of the women, which has lasted much longer than that of the men. The men in both areas wore a thick brown coat and, among other headgear, a typical brimmed hat with a squat crown—the 'mushroom hat'. Hempen or linen trousers and shirt were worn and bast shoes. The bast shoes, made of plaited bark, were widely worn in Poland, Russia and Finland before the dress developed more sophistication. There is a Polish saying to the effect that one can climb a tree without shoes and come down again with a new pair! The women's dress of the Green Forest made use of striped and checked homespun materials for skirts, aprons and capes and also skirts of plain material edged with ribbon worn with a white apron, or sometimes with an additional striped apron on top. A white blouse, embroidered on cuffs, shoulders and collar, was worn with a sleeveless bodice, either waist length or with a basque cut in four tabs leaving a gap at the front. Sleeved jackets, or longer jackets called *kaftany* or *sukmanki*, were worn according

65

to the weather or occasion. The usual Kurpie headdress is a kerchief folded over and over to leave a corner large enough to cover the crown, and tied behind. The ceremonial headdress of the girls, familiar to the audiences of the Dance Company, is the *czółka*, a tall stiff tiara with ribbons and a panache of flowers and feathers on the side. Although the men's dress had disappeared by the end of the nineteenth century, the women's dress could still be seen in the remotest areas well after the Second World War.

The southern part of Małopolska is dominated by the style of Cracow, even in parts outside Austrian Poland. This was the chief city of the region and was looked to as the chief centre of Polish national culture. Areas in between Cracow and those we have seen, for instance round Krzczonów or Sandomierż, show characteristics transitional between the two.

The Cracow dress does not survive except for organised festivities. The most famous place in the area for folk dress is the village of Bronowice which received particular attention from intellectuals interested in the Romantic Revival at the end of the nineteenth century. The dress of the men here is well known, consisting of a long sleeveless coat in navy blue

58 Kurpie region. Girls from Puszcza Biała—the White Forest. Twentieth century.

66

with braided and embroidered edges and corners and with tassels on the chest over a white shirt, a white belt with rows of metal discs on cords draped over the hip, red and white striped trousers and black boots. In other neighbourhoods the trousers have blue stripes. The best known of the various hats and caps is the square crowned *rogatywka,* trimmed with lambskin and for festive occasions with peacock feathers. This cap, here worn with a red crown, is to be found over much of Poland and appears to relate to similar caps worn in Scandinavia. Elsewhere the crown may be blue. Besides the *rogatywka,* another cap, seen also over a wide area of Małopolska, is the round knitted one of millstone shape. There are two

59 Girl from Bronowice in the Cracow region.

main styles of overcoat: a light summer one of simple cut and the special *kerezja* with full skirts and a triangular collar, found in a number of colours in the neighbourhood of Cracow.

The bodices of the women's dress in the Cracow region vary in style. Some are of extremely simple cut but others, most characteristic, have many overlapping tabs at the back created by the cut of the bodice in narrow panels. Those at the front are sewn on separately. The colouring of the Cracow dress was highly developed, especially at Bronowice. Elsewhere, flowered patterns might suffice, but at Bronowice, not only would flowered skirts and patterned or lace aprons be worn, but the

60 Kurpie region. Women from Puszcza Zielona—the Green Forest. Contemporary.

61 Region of Cracow. The character of 'Wiesław' from the novel of the same name, 1857.

bodice was trimmed with many rows of braid, embroidery and beads, as well as tassels. Several necklaces were also worn. Red boots, or black ones with red laces, tight to the leg, were the footwear for festive occasions. Shawls ranged from light flowered ones to brightly coloured plaids.

To the east the district of Rzeszów developed a style of its own, very different from the more primitive styles of south east Poland which are related to those of the Ukraine. In certain elements, the Rzeszów styles reflect those to the north and west, although the local embroidery is very individual.

The southern border of Poland is mountainous and the dress of the mountain inhabitants is related to that of the countries on the other side of the border. The area with the strongest surviving tradition is that of Podhale in the Polish Tatras. From the middle of the nineteenth century the Tatras were developed as a tourist resort, more particularly as a cultural resort, frequented by individuals in search of the true Poland, and the local folk traditions were much admired. The town of Zakopane grew in importance for this very reason and continues as a popular resort today, though with other attractions, including winter sports. Still, the folk tradition remains alive and on Corpus Christi day, for example, the local inhabitants parade in their dresses. The styles here, though similar to those of other localities in the mountains, are quite unlike the ones to be found outside the mountain range. The white wool trousers and coats of the men, the short sheepskin jackets, the wide belts and black hats, are very like those of neighbouring Slovakia. The women favour patterned skirts and bodices and wide-collared blouses with eyelet embroidery.

In Western Poland, for long part of German territory but now regained, one of the most interesting areas for folk dress is Lower Silesia. Unfortunately, it has not been worn for nearly a hundred years. The most remarkable item was the cap of the women which developed a great many varieties, recognizably related to other caps worn widely in Europe and significantly in neighbouring Bohemia. Here the basic shapes seem to have been deliberately exaggerated, front edges being deeply peaked and curved and lace edges more stiffly frilled. In this area also, the men adopted the *rogatywka* style of cap, but of a taller shape and with a turned down front peak. This resembles the helmet of a lancer as worn in so many European armies, often called by the name of *czapka,* the general Polish word for cap.

Norway

For geographical and also cultural reasons, motivated by political events in the nineteenth century, Norway is a particularly rewarding example of a country with a continuing tradition of folk dress. The formidable landscape and coastline of the country and the small population, meant that the communities were small and isolated. Indeed, even villages were few; getting to church or to see one's neighbours meant travelling, often by water. In Norway and also in Sweden church boats were a feature of Sunday church-going. It was often the parish community, collecting in this manner, which shared a style of dress.

When, in 1814, an international treaty delivered Norway from rule by Denmark, instead of the hoped for independence she found herself united to Sweden, though as a separate kingdom with a reasonable constitution.

62 Young people from Setesdal. Contemporary photograph.

In fact independence was not won until 1905, so throughout the nineteenth century Norwegian culture was proudly promoted as a boost to national pride. As elsewhere in Europe national pride included pride in the role played by ordinary people. In Norway society divided into two main classes, not upper and lower, but parallel. In the towns were the educated and mercantile class: members of modern European society in the fullest sense. In the countryside there was a yeoman rather than a peasant society: the *bönder* who, in prosperous areas like the Gudbrandsdal, had considerable property, if not much spare cash, so that they were more or less self sufficient. This was the class of people who wore local dress; the observers and recorders of it came from the cities. There were, naturally, poorer members of society also; sub-tenants and servants to the *bönder* and in the north, the Lapps, who, it appears, were treated as an inferior race.

There are a number of accounts of visits to Norway and Sweden written in English, from early in the nineteenth century onwards. These give excellent descriptions of life and conditions in the countryside and, in fact, often describe the political and economic condition of the country.

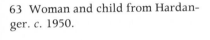

63 Woman and child from Hardanger. *c.* 1950.

Most of them are more generous with descriptions of household comfort or lack of it than with precise details of the folk dress, but they all mention it. Samuel Laing, who lived in Norway for two years in the 1830s, was well aware of, but did not subscribe to, the movement to preserve the dress which was apparently already threatened with decline. '... with all deference to the ingenious travellers who find it instructive to paint and describe local costumes, the tastes and wants which abolish them are the spurs to commerce, industry and civilisation: and their advance in a country, a much more important object of curiosity, than the forms of dress which they are superseding'. W. H. Breton, from New Zealand, travelling in Norway at the same time, hardly mentioned the dress and did not express much enthusiasm for what he saw. Like other travellers, he was appalled by the dirt, yet included as a supplement to his book a collection of prints of folk dress published by G. Prahl of Bergen, with the address from which they might be obtained. Richard Lovett, travelling with a party, including a photographer, in the 1880s, was more detailed in his descriptions. By this time the Norwegian Touring Club had come into being and the tourist trade was considerable. The Lapps were already one of the sights. Lovett describes a settlement near Tromsö. Judging by faces he recognized, he supposed that the Lapps had had to hurry back to the camp from Tromsö to be there before the visitors.

From the 1800s onwards was the period when Norwegian artists and observers were making their records, from which a number of nineteenth century publications take their material. The first book of illustrations to appear was by J. H. Senn: *Norsk nationale klaederdragter,* containing plates after paintings by the artist J. F. L. Dreier.

There were a number of important artists also taking inspiration for their studio pictures from Norwegian folk life, some directly, some from the work of their colleagues. Among them were Frich and Eckersberg, and the great Norwegian artist, Adolph Tideman, 1814–1876, who painted a series representing the various stages of a peasant's life. All these artists were contributing to the romantic spirit which inspired the revival of national culture, here as elsewhere.

Norway has contrived to keep a proportion of her folk dress intact to the present, in recent years with the aid of a movement to revive that which had been lost and even to create new styles. Formerly, a particular style might belong to a valley, or the shores of a fjord, or be shared by people attending the same church, groupings natural to the life, landscape and means of communication. Revived or created styles often apply to a wider area. It is usual to divide the country into east and west as there is a fairly clear distinction between the styles of each, those of the interior being freer in their colour schemes and also in their form than those of the coastal area. The latter are mostly black and white, relieved with bright colour, often red. The fashions themselves also have a family resemblance.

The main route through the interior from Oslo to the northern towns runs through the Gudbrandsdal. In winter this was also the main route to Sweden, over the frozen fjeld. This valley was always the most prosperous part of Norway and the dress there developed a richness in accordance with this prosperity. Incidentally, it is in the upper Gudbrandsdal, near to the Dovre Fjeld, where the action of Ibsen's Peer Gynt is set. The men's dress, not in use in recent times, was the long eighteenth century style of coat and breeches, much like that worn elsewhere in Europe. The women's dress has survived, but has also been given a boost by its

64 Bride from western Norway. Nineteenth century.

65 Woman from Vågå, upper Gudbrandsdal. Contemporary photograph. This is one of the few areas of Norway where the wearing of folk dress has been continuous without the benefit of revival.

72

popularity as a representative dress for the country to rival that of Hardanger. Though somewhat uniform in its components, it has many variations of detail. The festive dress is rather different in character from that of everyday. The bodice of the festive dress is often red or pink and may be of wool or silk woven or embroidered with bold flowers. It fastens up without a plastron, but the top few inches have no fastening which causes it to part in two points. The white blouse, simply cut from straight pieces, may be embroidered in white and trimmed with white tatting, with a little frill at the neck. The skirt is full with flat pleats. One, formerly in the possession of the author, was of thick blue wool embroidered with scattered sprigs of roses. Others are striped or checked or embroidered on top of a woven pattern in a most elaborate way. The apron, when worn, is dark and may also have coloured embroidery. Similar types may be seen in Romsdal which, though in West Norway, connects with Gudbrandsdal. Here, though, the apron will probably be white after the manner of western Norway, the embroidery more formalized and the blouse unfrilled. The everyday dress of Gudbrandsdal is, by contrast, a striped skirt and frequently a red checked bodice with a starched white kerchief over the head. A dark jacket may be worn also.

The dress which has survived most intact, however, is that of Setesdal, a valley in the south of Norway, not easy of access in former times. Not that that prevented all the visitors to Norway from going there and describing how isolated it was. The dress which is worn by men and women to this day is quite individual in outline. The length and proportion of the garments is unusual. From a high waist the wide pleated skirt of the women billows out, reaching hardly further than the knee. The top seam is folded inwards at the front so that the fullness hangs in two curves with a fold between, rather like wide trousers. The everyday dress is white with three black stripes on the edge. The Sunday dress is black with red and green edges, of the same shape but shorter. It is not worn separately but over the top of the everyday garment which shows below it. The dark bodice has green edges held together with silver chains. Large silver brooches of traditional design are also worn, for Setesdal is renowned for silver jewelry made locally in the valley, unlike the silver ornaments of the west coast which are mostly factory made in Bergen. Black and red kerchiefs, rolled at the front, cover the head. A shawl called the *tjeld,* usually striped, is worn about the shoulders out of doors. The men wear high bibbed trousers, coming up under the armpits and extremely short jackets which allow the decorated trouser bib to show. Patches are worn on the seat as decoration. This attire is not particularly ancient, dating from the early nineteenth century. An illustration in Tønsberg shows a bridegroom dressed in the old style with a waist-length red waistcoat fastened only at the waist over a sleeved jacket. The trousers are the baggy breeches often seen in older peasant dress and at one time general in Norway. He is also wearing a splendid belt of brass ornaments mounted close together.

The style of female dress, which hangs from a small yoke or braces, is not confined to Agder and the vicinity of Setesdal, but nowhere else is it so short. It is to be found in Telemark also and has spread throughout Hallingdal. The modern Hallingdal dress is of this kind, in fact, an ancient style though possibly brought to the fore by the fashionable high waists of Napoleonic times. In this case it is adapted to use modern bright colours in its accessories and trimmings, unusual for peasant dress, including a

66 Bride and married woman from Voss, Hordaland. Middle of the nineteenth century. The bride's headdress is worn only here and in western Telemark. As in neighbouring Hardanger there is still a strong, though revived, tradition of local dress.

74

complicated headdress with coloured fringes. This best dress, like that of Setesdal, is worn over the top of the everyday garment. The first plate in Tønsberg, taken from an original by Frich, shows a couple in the 'old style' from Naes in Hallingdal. The woman is shown in a dark red bodice and skirt, the bodice widely trimmed at the front where it gapes open to reveal heavy silver jewelry. Her close black cap is bound with coloured ribbon and a frill of lace frames her face. She wears a long apron of bought calico which Tønsberg grudgingly allows, taking however, the opportunity to deplore the taste of women who wear the new-fangled dress of bought fabrics which he considers tawdry. Yet the Hallingdal dress is praised above others for its artistry by modern writers. The man in the picture wears an ample grey homespun jacket, embroidered yellow breeches of the kind for which Hallingdal was famous and a red stitched skull cap, one of the kinds of male headdress of the older type seen in various localities. Elsewhere in Norway long coats were worn but, eventually, in most areas a short jacket, sometimes very short, came into favour, until eventually modern town fashions took over. Thereafter, except for Setesdal, men's folk dress is met with only in revived form.

In western Norway the women's dress has a fairly consistent character in that the colour schemes are limited and the pattern of the embroidery is usually geometrical rather than baroque. The styles derive ultimately from the seventeenth century and are, in fact, the undress styles to be seen almost everywhere in Western European folkdress, where a bodice or corselet is worn to show. Some of the Norwegian bodices originally extended over the hips in tabs but this feature was soon lost. Though in some districts the bodice fronts have fastening chains, they do not look especially corset-like; the cut is too low to be functional and the wide plastron inserted into the opening acts as a decorative panel; it does not project or have any function as a busk.

67 Girls dressing their hair before going into church after arrival by boat, 1885.

Western Norway is renowned for its white embroidery, the Hardanger work being best known. Related techniques are used almost everywhere and are shown to good effect on the white aprons over plain dark pleated skirts. Since so much of the decoration is centred on the bodice, most of the effect is lost if a sleeved jacket is worn. This applies to some extent also to eastern Norway, especially with everyday wear. No doubt the extremely short jackets of southern Norway are a conscious means of avoiding this.

The best known style of western Norway, and indeed of the whole country, is that of Hardanger. It has changed little since the early nineteenth century except that the waist has come to its natural level from being rather high. The skirt, which earlier was dark blue, is now black and the bodice usually red, though it may be in other colours also. The embroidery on the plastron is now of beadwork, whereas formerly it was worked in wool. The oblong bonnet, sometimes worn by young girls, has its square ends also beaded. The white apron has a panel of the open work embroidery typical of Hardanger. The white pleated *skaut* or headdress is worn only by older women. Many of the other styles of Hordaland—there are as many as twenty—resemble the Hardanger style. The dress of Voss to the north is remarkably similar though the skirt is trimmed with velvet and the *skaut* is a triangular embroidered kerchief, kept to a stiff shape by starch and a leather foundation.

In Norway, as in the rest of Scandinavia, the bridal headdress is usually a crown, not merely a chaplet but sometimes an actual crown of metal, usually silver gilt; at other times a decorated stiffened shape. Most brides borrow their crown from the parish, but some families possess their own as an heirloom. The Voss bridal headdress is different. It lies across the top of the head and the decorations hang from the projecting side pieces. This style is also worn in Telemark.

The folk dress of Norway today is the result of a revival movement given impetus towards the end of the nineteenth century by the foundation of handcraft societies, not only here but elsewhere in Scandinavia. The word *bunad*, meaning a revived folk dress, has come into use and in Norway we have the only state aided committee in Scandinavia for regulating the revival of folk dress; maybe the only one in Europe outside the Socialist countries. I owe the information I have on it to Aagot Noss. The committee, *Landsnemnda for bunadsspørsmål*: State Committee for folk dress revival, was founded in 1947 and is at present working to a constitution dating from 1967. Its purpose is to give advice on revival and reconstruction on the foundation of traditional styles and thus to minimise the likelihood of illfounded and fanciful creations.

68 The old dress of Naes in Hallingdal from Tønsberg's *Norske Nationaldragter, 1852*.

Sweden

The domestic arts and decorative crafts have an ancient and continuous tradition in Sweden. For hundreds of years woodwork, metalwork and textiles have been employed in the home for decorative as well as utilitarian purposes, and to this tradition belongs also the art of the folkdress. Moreover, an awareness of the function of dress in society has a long history in Sweden, so that by the time King Gustav III was making his attempt to create a national costume in the eighteenth century, the peasant dress with separate local styles was well established, and over a long period had been remarked on in government reports and parish minutes.

As always, the rulers and administrators were concerned with the appropriateness of the dress worn by different classes of society. We have met sumptuary laws in most countries, but in Sweden this concern was accompanied by a genuine interest in discovering and maintaining the local styles, a concern which came to most other countries somewhat later. We find parish priests not only condemning their flocks for unsuitable dress, but also for adopting items which properly belonged to other parishes. We find landowners in the eighteenth and nineteenth centuries designing fashions for their tenants though with only moderate success. Enthusiasts for dress as an expression of national culture, of which there were many in nineteenth century Sweden among the intellectual classes, assumed for their own wear versions of reformed dress, in particular reviving knee breeches after trousers had superseded them.

In the end, however, it was the styles which had evolved naturally, absorbing changes which suited them, which persisted longest, and which provided the foundation for the modern revival movement based on historically correct examples.

Authors and artists provided a record of folk life in Sweden from early in the nineteenth century, the first illustrated book being, *Ett år i Sverige,* (The year in Sweden), the illustrations engraved by C. Forsell from originals by the artist J. G. Sandberg. Then in the middle of the century, during a period of great interest in genre painting based on folk themes, a number of books of lithographed plates appeared, produced notably by A. O. Hård and C. A. Dahlström. Yet during this very period, the dresses themselves were beginning to disappear and it was the consciousness of this which made the tradition more precious to its intellectual guardians and eventually prompted active participation. In 1874 an arts and crafts movement, related to that started in Britain by William Morris, found fertile soil in Sweden and the various homecrafts (hemslöjd) were vigorously revived, bringing new life to the wearing of folk dress. At this time, Artur Hazelius began, with his assistants, to tour the country in search of material to form the collection of the Northern Museum and the open air museum at Skansen, both of which he founded. Thus, not only were specimens preserved, but correct examples were made available to counteract the fanciful confections which were beginning to appear as 'national dress'. The work is continued through agencies still active today.

The region which kept its folk dress longest was Dalecarlia (Dalarna) not, as might be expected, a remote area but a prosperous region of central Sweden where no doubt prosperity brought with it a conservative taste. It was from this area that the first examples to be studied were found and in which today most active use is made of the revived dress. Parishes round Lake Siljan; Leksand, Rättvik, Floda and Gagnef provide good examples of Dalecarlian dress and we might profitably look at the first two. It should not be supposed that they only had one style each; there were a number of variations according to season, occasion, purpose and status, in the formal wear quite apart from occupational dress. In this respect, the church calendar was of fundamental importance in that it provided the occasions calling for special attire. Leksand, an important parish with a visiting congregation coming from afar by boat and other means, used to have a complete ritual of colours to be worn according to the season of the almanac as well as garments suitable for the weather. The general outline of the ensemble was fairly constant; a black skirt, formerly pleated but later plain, a laced bodice, a neck-cloth pinned to lie in two points on the breast, a cap, either bonnet shaped or hood-shaped, a cloth jacket for summer and a suede jacket and warm hood for winter, and, above all, the apron, which provided the basis for the colour change and its name. While the everyday or ordinary Sunday apron was brightly striped, solemn feast days and fasts and, of course, mourning required a sober dress. Other church festivals required red, green or blue aprons and the appropriate adjustment of accessories as prescribed. Rather typical as decoration are red pompoms, worn on the ties to the shoes, to men's breeches at the knee and elsewhere, also the red piping on the dark jackets and coats.

Such decorations are also found in the dress of Rättvik, but otherwise the dress gives a somewhat different impression, rather individual among the parishes of Dalecarlia. Here the woman's apron with bold horizontal stripes is not separate but forms the front of the skirt. The stripes are usually red, green, yellow and white. The back of the skirt may be dark blue or bright blue with a green edge. The short laced bodice may be covered with a black jacket trimmed in red. The printed cotton fichu is folded and pinned more narrowly than in Leksand. Married women have a hood-shaped pointed cap trimmed with lace, but the girl's black cap has a special style, almost Phrygian shaped in two sections, piped with red at the join and finished with red ribbons ending in pompoms behind. A white cap is worn under it. The red stockings are required to be baggy over the ankle. The men's attire, also employing dark blue frieze for coat and waistcoat, has its own eccentricities with trousers, not only short in the waist to reveal an expanse of shirt, but light coloured above the knee and dark below it. Straps at the knee are decorated with hanging red pompoms, as is the hat band. Red piping outlines the collarless coat and waistcoat, which is cut with epaulettes low on the shoulder.

At Häverö, in Uppland there is also an individual style. There is in Sweden and Finland a widespread fashion for caps which consist of a stiff, casque-like, bonnet crown, rather close with a bow behind and with an 'undercap' of lace showing on the forehead which is, in fact, only an edging tucked into the front of the cap. At Häverö, this cap has a special shape, rising high and square behind the head. Both the buttoned

69 Scania, Järrestad. Nineteenth century. From Racinet, 1888. The breast-plate-like brooches are to be seen elsewhere in Scania also.

waistcoat and laced jacket are cut in a rising line behind so that the chemise shows above the waistline of the skirt. Red and green striped materials are much in use at Häverö. The men's dress is of rather formal cut.

In Hälsingland, at Delsbo, near the east coast, an attractive use was made of knitted garments, for both men and women. A girl would wear a blue, or later, black skirt with an edging of applied red cloth, a blue apron striped with lighter blue and white on a broad red and white band with two red tassels. The sleeveless bodice was red, finely striped, the edges hooking together. Her knitted jacket fastened to one side to form a square neckline and was boldly patterned all over in black and red with additions of green and white. The stiff cap was covered with toning patterned cotton and had a bow at the back. Unusually for this form of headdress girls often let their hair hang loosely. The red stockings were earlier of red cloth, not made to fit, but were later knitted. The men wore light coloured leather or blue cloth breeches and blue stockings, a shirt with the collar standing high tied round with a silk scarf and a blue jacket with silver buttons, or he might wear a brightly coloured knitted jacket, like that of the girl. With it he would wear a round sectional cap with black binding on the seams. There was also a long white coat of older collarless cut.

Södermanland is a region just to the south west of Stockholm, yet surprisingly contains a style at Vingåker which harks back to an early period. The rather simple everyday dress of the women comprises a skirt, long apron, high sleeveless bodice and sleeved jacket, both rather short and only fastening at top and bottom. The headdress is a large square starched cloth folded diagonally with the long ends tied round the head, the rest standing out stiffly like a nurse's square. The festival dress, however, is of a style to be met with here and there all over Europe, wherein the skirt hangs from just below the shoulders, from a minute yoke. The sleeved jacket is only long enough to buckle over this tiny bodice and the apron has a narrow panel on the breast from which it hangs in gathers, trapped by a belt at the waist. The strange headdress is of ribbons, wound round a foundation, with a circular attachment on the crown of coiled red ribbon bound over a core of flax. The men's dress, which ordinarily has a short plain dark jacket, acquires a long white collarless one for festival wear.

We have already encountered the products of different periods of development, sometimes together in the same locality or even dress. Cloth stockings, sectional caps, a smockline dress and straight collarless coats of simple cut belong to an early period. Coats with a shaped cut and epaulettes, certain typical caps and headdresses, derive from a period no later than the early seventeenth century. One could point out in other localities colour schemes belonging to the period of rococo. Men's formal styles often belong to the eighteenth and early nineteenth century. However, when we come to the provinces, to the west towards Denmark, and the rest of Europe we find the influence of the Renaissance, reinforced and more firmly established than elsewhere, owing to early influences from that direction. Yet we also see in several localities, for example, Ingelstad and Järrestad in Scåne (Scania) the taste for coiled flat headdresses rather like that worn with a fundamentally different style at Vingåker. Both at Järrestad and Ingelstad heavy jewelry is a feature of the women's dress, and with the wedding dress in particular. At Ingelstad not only are the gilded silver plates on red cloth backgrounds worn on each

70 Couple from Ierfsö in Halland, from E. Forsell's *Ett År i Sverige*, 1827.

side above the waist, but one or two large crosses are worn as pendants. The belt of red cloth also has metal plates mounted on it with two long ends hanging to the hem of the knee-length coat. The bridegroom wears a shirt specially made and embroidered for him by the bride, sometimes begun in childhood to get it done in time. The short jackets of the men in Scåne fasten high with a long row of brass buttons, as do the waistcoats. Light leather breeches or white linen trousers are worn. The collars of men's shirts and women's blouses are rather wide and often worn standing rather than turned down.

The styles of Halland, farther up the west coast, also have mixed origins with a strong flavour of the Renaissance in cut but with colour schemes of a later time. At Årstad, however, the men wear jackets with short tails and waistcoats with high collars in the style of the early nineteenth century. The early picture from Ierfsö by Forsell is interesting, particularly for the style of cap worn by the woman—very deep and curved, and the long tunics with armholes so wide that they are almost backless, worn by both the man and the woman in apparently identical style.

Poland. Bride and groom from the east of Cracow
Polen. Braut und Bräutigam aus der Gegend von Krakau
Pologne. Marié et mariée de l'est de la région de Cracovie

Norway. Couple from Telemark
Norwegen. Paar aus Telemark
Norvège. Couple de Telemark

Sweden. Man and woman from Häverö. 19th century
Schweden. Mann und Frau aus Häverö. 19. Jahrhundert
Suède. Villageois et villageoise de Häverö. XIXᵉ siècle

Finland. Man and woman from Karelia. 19th century
Finnland. Mann und Frau aus Karelien. 19. Jahrhundert
Finlande. Paysan et paysanne de la Carélie. XIXe siècle

Finland

71 A Finnish peasant as depicted in William Coxes' *Travels*, 1785.

The Republic of Finland has come into the modern world with great speed. Born in strife, she has had only the years since the Second World War to develop properly, yet the preparation for independence was taking place throughout the nineteenth century. At this time she was a separate Grand Duchy under the rule of Russia, responsible for her own administration until the last years when Russian policy changed and Finnish nationalism was threatened. At the beginning of the period the Swedish language and culture prevailed. Now, the reversal is complete and Swedish speakers are in a small minority.

Unfortunately, for our purpose, the change to modern dress is also complete. The rise of Finnish culture in the nineteenth century, as reflected in the dress, built upon the suggestions and example of King Gustav III of Sweden, 1746–1792. He laid the foundation of a national dress for the territories under his rule and, as in other countries, regional differences were developed. By the 1870s, the foundations of ethnographical study were firmly established and examples of regional dress were collected for a national exhibition of Finnish folk arts.

Finnish folk dress is divided into two main kinds; those of Swedish influence, that is the western Finnish styles, and those of Karelia and eastern Finland. In fact, this geographical division is not exact, as in eastern Finland, there are also styles influenced by Sweden. The Karelian styles are related to those of Russia and Eastern Europe.

The western style for the women is basically like that of other areas of western Europe, with a bodice and skirt over a chemise and with jackets and other top garments worn in addition. Finland was never in the main a feudal society and at an early date there was sufficient prosperity for the use of a certain amount of bought material for important garments and for professional tailors to be employed for the heavy clothes. At the same time, the ordinary, everyday clothes were homespun and woven, as elsewhere, from hemp, flax and wool and, as elsewhere also, the parts which showed were made of finer material or more elaborately decorated than those which were hidden. The chemise, or smock for instance, though sewn into one garment was nevertheless made of different materials in its different parts, usually a hard-wearing hempen lower half and a fine bodice part and sleeves which could be renewed or replaced, of which a supply would be worked for the trousseau. The overskirt might be of good quality bought material, often plain red and much valued, or dark blue or black. Alternatively, it might be of homespun striped material, usually worn with the stripes vertical, a fashion imitated from the modes of the seventeenth and eighteenth centuries when striped silks were much worn. Aprons, if worn at all, might also be homespun, sometimes matching the skirt exactly, or they might be of bought patterned calico. Headdresses were of two kinds, either the small shaped cap of patterned material usually with a frill, in the Swedish style, or a kerchief.

The men's attire from western Finland dates back to the eighteenth century and before, being an adaptation of fashionable styles. The Reverend William Coxe, travelling in the 1780s, observed how much more prosperous the Finns were than their Russian counterparts and included an engraving of a peasant in winter dress. The cloth garments worn in warmer seasons show the standing collars, both to the jacket and coat, and the rather straight cut of the eighteenth century. They did not reach the next natural development of fashion; the wider lapels and turned down collar until late, though the breeches developed into trousers. As revived in the twentieth century by folk dancers, the dress often reverts to knee

72 Married woman from Koivisto, a parish in the Karelian Isthmus, photographed in 1914.

73 Married women: Ruokolahti (left)—Joutseno (right)—parishes in Southern Karelia. Nineteenth century.

breeches worn with a jacket of more modern cut. The most active agency for the revival in the twentieth century is the Braga Society, which since 1906 has worked to preserve the Swedish folk culture of Finland, literary and artistic. In 1922 and 1923, the Society held meetings to lay down rules for the reconstruction of local dresses and since 1952 has published instructions for making them. Instruction is also given in folk dancing. There is no similar society supporting the Finnish speaking revival movement but attempts are made to encourage folk culture in general.

In eastern Finland the Karelian folk culture reflects that of neighbouring Russia and the dress also is related to it rather than to western Europe.

74 Married couple from central Finland. The woman is specifically from Mántyharju parish. Nineteenth century.

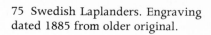

75 Swedish Laplanders. Engraving dated 1885 from older original.

So in the north we have a dividing line between east and west such as we have already encountered in Southern Europe. The Karelian dress survived longer as a natural tradition than the western styles, but since it went out of use has not been revived so actively. The basis of the women's dress is the *sarakko* related to the Russian *sarafan*. This garment was of dark, homespun wool with a border of coloured cloth. The smock had a decorative front panel with the opening immediately to the side. Coats of linen or wool, according to season, formed the outer wear. The headdress was a white veil or, in some districts in bad weather, a square of striped wool cloth equipped with a strap might be worn over the head; otherwise it was worn hanging from the shoulder. An important accessory was the decorated belt or girdle carrying a sheath knife, needlecase and purse. Male Karelian dress retained the ancient form of trousers rather than the fashionable breeches, over which was worn a loose coat of angular cut crossed over and girded on the outside rather like a dressing gown. Under it the shirt, worn as a top garment in summer, hung over the trousers. A long cloak was worn as an additional outer garment. The colour of these garments was originally light as they were made of undyed fabrics, but later dyed fabrics were employed. Headgear was of various shapes in cloth and knitted wool and, in winter, of fur. The tall, top-hat like style was confined to western Finland, as was the round-topped knitted style.

76 Lapp woman with child in typical cradle. Nineteenth century.

The Lapps

The Lapps are a people living in the north of Norway, Sweden, Finland and the Kola Peninsula in the Soviet Union. They are separate in race from their neighbours and with a language and culture of their own. If not indigenous to their present territory it would appear that they have come from nearby Asia at a very early date. Their language has survived official indifference and disapproval—education has usually been in the main

77 Shore Laplander of Norway in winter dress. From *Travels through Sweden, Norway and Finmark* by A. de Capell Brooke, 1823.

language of the country until recent, in Norway very recent, times. Their culture, on the other hand, in spite of a revival connected with the growth of Lapp national consciousness, is now dying out as the result of the encroachment of modern life. In the USSR, the Lapps are integrated into the system and the reindeer herds are nationalized.

The Lapp culture has been reported by observers since the beginning of the Christian era and from early times the people have been visited by missionaries. In fact, the Lutheran, Catholic and Orthodox churches all have their adherents. Most of the early reports are by missionaries. From the eighteenth century, illustrated accounts have been fairly numerous. The skill of the Lapps as huntsmen and fishermen, their prowess on skis, their dependence on the herds of reindeer are all well known. Their way of life was adapted to the means of livelihood, whether nomadic or settled. Their clothes accordingly have been adapted to suit the climate and lifestyle.

Because of the climate, rather hot in summer and extremely cold in winter, the clothing is seasonal, basically of skins and fur with wool linings in winter, and homespun smocks and trousers in summer. The dress still survives for special occasions, though now many ready made garments are worn. The traditional styles have changed little since the end of the eighteenth century.

The summer smocks or tunics are typically dark, often blue in colour, with decorative bands of coloured cloth and metallic embroidery, the colours denoting different districts of origin. The women's garments are fuller than the men's with more inserted panels. The trousers are of ingenious cut with no seam in the fork. The metallic embroidery of pewter, a traditional craft which had died out, has been revived as a folk art in recent years. The silver ornaments, of which many may be worn at a time, were usually bought, but now silver work has also been adopted as a craft as part of the interest in reviving the old traditions.

The caps of the men and bonnets of the women give the Lapp dress much of its characteristic appearance. Changes have taken place over a period and in different regions but the basic pattern is consistent through the nineteenth century. The men's are almost always sectional caps either more or less conical, or flattened in the crown. Early in the nineteenth century there was a style where the crown had a square shape with four corners which, with modifications, still survives in Norway. The illustrations in Knut Leem's *Beskrivelse over Finnmarkens Lapper*, (Description of the Finnmark Lapps) 1767, show the women wearing strange bobbin shaped hats with flat tops. The paintings of Johannes Flintoe, done at Karasjok in the early nineteenth century, show the women in the oddly shaped bonnets with a high extension on the crown which appears to be a development from the style in Leem. This forward pointing projection was stiffened with a hollow wooden shaper. The style was worn until late in the century. The bonnets worn more recently are adaptations, either close fitting in the crown or with soft full crowns. The men in Flintoe's pictures wear the square crowned cap. The red tassel, sometimes to be seen on the men's conical caps, has developed to a very large size, a feature which has become rather typical.

78 Lapp couple from Knud Leem's *Account of the Laplanders of Finmark,* 1767.

Denmark

Denmark with its strategic geographical position was the first of the Scandinavian countries to prosper in the modern world. Consequently, its folk dress fell into disuse more than a hundred years ago, except for a few localities, and has never been revived in the systematic way that it has elsewhere in Scandinavia. It is, however, worn as a conscious revival by folk dance societies under the aegis of *Foreningen til Folkedansens Fremme*, the Union for the Furtherance of Folk Dance. In this work the Union has the co-operation of the National Museum in preparing authentic patterns for the reconstructed dresses.

The geography of Denmark with a small population engaged in agriculture and fishing on a number of islands and the Jutland Peninsula provided suitable conditions for the development of separate styles in the different areas. In a few such localities, for various reasons, the dress lasted longer than elsewhere. For instance, on the island of Fanø in the North Sea, the women's dress was worn until comparatively recently, though even twenty five years ago none of the wearers was under seventy years old. The Fanø dress is rather distinctive, though the people of other nearby islands once wore similar styles. Dark colours were favoured in matching patterns. Thus a dress might have a woollen skirt, pleated for best, and jacket and apron matching each other in patterned calico. Likewise, the headscarf and top neckerchief would match, being often reddish or brown or, for mourning, blue or purple. The headscarf was tied closely over an undercap so that no hair was revealed and the ends were knotted on top. This uncompromising severity did not preclude a show of vanity—Fanø women used to affect a special swinging gait and they also protected their complexions against sand and sun with face masks which, one trusts, revealed some improvement when removed.

There are other areas where the dress survived longer on the main island of Zealand. One example is that of the market women in the fish market of Copenhagen, coming in from nearby Skovshoved, wearing green skirts with stiff white kerchiefs. Formerly they were joined by peasant women from the market gardens of Amager, but they ceased to wear local dress early in the century. The market gardeners of Amager, like those of Vierlande serving the city of Hamburg in Germany, were of Dutch origin and this could be seen in their dress. The fine clothes of the women, particularly, indicated prosperity, with dark textures and rich embroidery. The men's attire was rather odd, owing its effect to the shaggy blue hat of great size and weight and the large number of baggy garments worn together.

In contrast to the areas so surprisingly near to Copenhagen which kept their dress so late, the other district in Zealand in which it survived into the early twentieth century was the western peninsula of Røsnœs. Here, a rigid etiquette ruled the colour scheme and the choice of garments to be

79 Fanø. Young woman in a face-mask as protection against wind and sand. The dress of Fanø became extinct in the 1960s.

worn on family occasions and seasons of the church calendar. A large
wardrobe was, therefore, required. A girl's trousseau represented a
considerable investment of time and money, a consideration which no
doubt helped the tradition to survive, as the dress would not lightly be
discarded. The best dress, often made use use of ribbons and bought
material in combination with the basic homespun and woven or knitted
fabrics. An example in the National Museum, worn for Whitsuntide and
weddings, shows a pretty silk cap with ribbons behind and under the chin,
a red patterned sleeveless bodice over a garment with knitted sleeves, a
tightly pleated red skirt with lighter bands and a checked apron.

80 Girl from Århus. Nineteenth
century.

This combination of garments, with local differences, is the usual one for the women's dress. There was a basic chemise, the top of which functioned as a blouse, a sleeveless fitted bodice, fastening or lacing in front, a pleated skirt and a large apron covering the front of the skirt. No doubt, because of the uncertain climate, it was the habit almost everywhere to wear a sleeved underbodice which was often knitted, or to have knitted or cloth sleeves inserted into the top bodice. The knitting was usually in a characteristic diamond pattern in self colour. When sleeves were short the chemise cuffs, perhaps embroidered, would show or undersleeves or knitted mittens might be worn. For dancing, or in

80a The red dress of Whitsuntide and weddings from Røsnœs, western Zealand.

warm weather, the under jacket could be discarded. A kerchief was generally worn, tucked into the top of the bodice.

Because the dress fell into disuse so early, many of the styles never progressed past the period of high waists belonging to the time of the Napoleonic Empire. Jackets worn over the bodice were of the spenser type, often with leg-of-mutton sleeves. In fact, Danish folk dress was extremely practical. Not only did it provide for layers to be added or removed—cloaks, capes and outer bonnets were also available—it also, while remaining simple, lent itself to festive wear by the use of finer materials and appropriate trimmings. The caps were the items above all which set off the dresses and which differentiated the status of the women, the occasion and the locality.

On the northern part of the island of Falster the women wore a headdress like a deep bonnet composed of a small silk cap from which projected a wide headband with lace edging to shade the face. This went well with the handsome dress often of dark rich material trimmed with wide ribbons with pleated edges.

On Laesö island between northern Jutland and Sweden the headdress was a swathed cloth or scarf, very medieval in appearance, and the dress which went with it was made of fine imported materials for best wear, decorated with heavy silver ornaments, also of ancient design.

Jutland has many interesting headdresses, employing more starched white material and lace then elsewhere. Laundered into elaborate styles, one would not have thought it practical for the local weather conditions. At Salling, the cap itself was small and worn at the back of the head, but there were large fans of stiff lace framing the face. At Århus the cap not only had side wings, but a starched white, lace-trimmed, triangular cloth, the point tucked down at the back. At Thisted the cap was a large pleated halo but also here, and more generally at Ringkøbing, the frilled cap was dominated by a large felt top hat, a style apparently confined to this part of Jutland.

The men's dress in Denmark was less differentiated according to district. Right up to the first decades of the nineteenth century the men continued to wear the long or short coat, the waistcoat and the breeches which came into fashion at the end of the seventeenth century. They were often made of striped homespun or bought cloth in imitation of the striped silks of the styles from which they derived. Such stripes were favoured throughout Scandinavia. The long coats, in later times at least, were worn only by older men for formal occasions, the broad hats, also worn, were very much in the style of the dress of the peasantry for formal occasions throughout Europe. Heads were always covered so the ordinary headwear was the knitted cap, usually red. In Jutland the hood, an ancient form of headcovering, survived as general wear, with a hat added on top if a formal occasion should arise. Red was favoured for the hood also.

In about 1830 there was a fairly rapid change of style, again reflecting the change in post revolutionary styles throughout Europe. Black clothes of a more modern cut, coats with lapels and long trousers instead of breeches began to be worn. The tall hat replaced the broad hat for formal wear. From this stage, so close to fashionable town dress, only a small step was required to leave the folk dress behind.

Iceland

In contrast to the rich variety of styles on the Scandinavian mainland, in Iceland there is no difference between one region of the country and another. For once the dress is truly national. There is not, after all, much scope for regional differences in a country with such a small population and with only a quarter of the land in active use. Moreover, in the last century, when the present dress was redesigned, the population was only about 70,000 and declining to the point where total depopulation seemed a possibility. However, independence from Denmark, partial at first and latterly complete, has altered the situation and given the Icelanders something to celebrate. It is, in fact, on Independence Day when the folk dress is most likely to be seen.

The folk dress worn today dates back to the 1860s when the Icelandic artist and antiquarian, Sigurdur Gudmundsson, redesigned it at a time when it was in decline. It is, in effect, his invention, though based on historical examples. At the time of this revival the dress was nevertheless still being worn in its old form, so there is a degree of overlap between the designed forms and the old dress which evolved in a continuous tradition. It is clear from illustrations that the new dress is not really a peasant dress

81 Illustration from *Travels in the Island of Iceland*, 1810, by Sir George Steuart Mackenzie.

at all, but is derived from burgher fashions. They evolved apparently along the lines of such attire but retained, well into the nineteenth century, several features of Renaissance fashion; the pendant belt and the flat stiff collar which was the successor to the ruff. The chief eccentricity was the headdress which, in earlier times, was bag-shaped or conical and curving over to the front, made up of cloths bound round the head and pinned. The culmination of that style is to be seen in the illustration by C. F. Lund, dated 1861, where the top part, formerly meant to stiffen the whole headdress inside, has become uncovered, its base bound into the turban-like head covering. Illustrations show this style up to the end of the century.

The festive dress designed by Sigurdur Gudmundsson is very like that shown by Lund. It is black, with the braid decoration replaced by elaborate embroidery. The flat collar is not retained. The new jacket is short and separate from the skirt, though in wear they are hooked together. It is designed to gape at the front to reveal a panel of white

82 Icelandic Lady of the eighteenth century. 1771.

embroidery. Above this the edges of the bodice are fastened by a brooch. The neckline and cuffs are edged with lace ruffles and the whole edge, that is, neck front and cuffs, has gold metallic embroidery on black velvet. The skirt is embroidered in silk round its lower part. The belt, or girdle, may be of metal links or embroidered. The designed headdress harks back to ancient examples. A white, curved pad is fastened on the head and covered with a white veil, while a gilded metal circlet fits round the front in a medieval looking way. In 1890 a pageant, or theatrical presentation, was held at Akureyri to celebrate the birth of the nation in the ninth century and similar headdresses were thought appropriate for the lady participants to wear in ninth century character. It is possible to wear a coloured dress with this headdress, but black is favoured most.

Another version of the dress, the jacket style, is also black and includes a longer jacket with a pleated basque at the back. With it a pleated skirt and a light or patterned apron is worn. The neckline is filled in with a scarf which fastens in a large bow at the front. This style derives much more directly from the everyday wear of ordinary people. Formerly it was much less uniform than now. The third version, worn today, very popular with younger people is an undress version, with a chained corselet over a white blouse, also worn with a light apron. In the past the corselet was worn under the sleeved jackets or under the gowns of the period which could be removed if wished; now one wears one style or the other. With the last two styles the formal headdress is not worn but a tasselled cap, nowadays of black velvet or silk. This was formerly knitted and originally adopted by the women for comfort and convenience from the ordinary knitted caps of the men, and not necessarily black. Its refinement has become so extreme that it has to be pinned in place to prevent the weight of the elongated tassel, joined on by a metal tube, from pulling it off.

A coloured plate in *Travels in the Island of Iceland during the summer of 1810*, by Sir George Steuart Mackenzie, illustrates a range of different styles and indicates that blue was a popular colour at the time and that bright trimmings were in favour.

The Netherlands

The Netherlands is a country of contrasts and contradictions. It has always shown two faces to the world; the colonial power engaged in world trade on the one hand, and the pastoral and agricultural country with its rural and parochial traditions on the other. For centuries it has been a centre of learning and a refuge for dissidents, yet is also a country of strong puritan traditions; tolerant to others, it is hard on itself. It occupies an open and accessible position in western Europe, yet until modern times internal communications were often difficult as many communities were isolated by water. It has maintained a strong tradition of folk dress, stronger than anywhere else in western Europe, yet its neighbours have lost theirs and, in the case of Belgium with which it was once united, there never was such a tradition. The reason for these contrasts must lie in the character of the people, enterprising yet deeply conservative. Indeed, the folk dress of the Netherlands reflects this. Its qualities are solid, its rules strict, its form rigid—even restricting, yet its details are rich and refined. Pins are used in quantities, exactly placed to keep the dress in order, yet the shape which they maintain may be one of great eccentricity. The caps are formidably starched and firmly positioned yet, as developed in recent years, they achieve that vivacity of style which can only be obtained by skill and worn with confidence.

All this contributes strongly to our impression of the Dutch character; the dress helps to form our view and, at the same time, the character of the people appears to conform to the style of the dress.

Unfortunately, the popular image abroad of Dutch folk dress seems to be that of Volendam and Marken to the exclusion of other districts. There is a grain of truth in this in that these are the two styles most likely to be encountered by visitors. They are certainly important surviving examples and need to be mentioned at some length, but they are not the only ones and in some ways are not typical. Neither of them, for instance, employs the metal head-clasp or *ear-iron* which is very general in other districts and very typical of Dutch folk dress. In the space at our disposal one cannot attempt to do justice to the rich variety of styles, past and present, but one can attempt to adjust the balance by mentioning a number of examples. One can also, at least, make clear the difference between the dress of Marken and Volendam. The style sometimes seen in advertisements and illustrations is nonsensical—long plaits with a winged cap, for instance, will not do.

Most of the styles have developed, as elsewhere, since the eighteenth century and those surviving are still evolving, though it is surprizing to what extent they are still recognizable. Most of the drastic changes have taken place in this century.

The oldest and most singular of the regional styles still surviving, is undoubtedly that of Marken. Although it has continued to evolve it

85 Staphorst. Indoor dress of young woman, worn without 'ear-iron' or outer cap. Twentieth century.

94

retains its early fundamental character to a remarkable extent. Maaskamp shows a plate with two examples and Bing has several illustrations which it is instructive to compare. A visitor in the 1880s, Richard Lovett, described the Marken dress very clearly from an outsider's viewpoint:

'The men wear a kind of closefitting vest or jacket of brown cloth, with double rows of buttons and a low collar. Buttoned to this, very often by large gold buttons—are wide baggy short trousers or knickerbockers. Dark brown or blue stockings, and sabots or shoes complete the costume. Generally they wear caps; but on Sundays and festivals they wear tall hats. Under the waistcoat is a red shirt, and when at work the men often throw off the waistcoat, and the red colour forms a bright contrast with the dull coloured boats and somewhat saddened landscape'.

86 Volendam. The *hul* as developed at the present day.

In more recent times the everyday top garment is a short, loose blue and white striped shirt. The formal jacket which replaces it is black. Lovett goes on to describe the women:

'The headdress is unlike anything to be seen in other parts of Holland. It is a large white cap, somewhat resembling a mitre in shape, adorned with lace and embroidery, which is shown up by means of a brown lining. On either side of the face a long thick curl of hair, generally false, hangs down, and sometimes the hair is also cut short on the forehead and trained to curl upward and backward (with soap). The body of the dress is sleeveless, usually brown and always covered with gay, richly coloured embroidery. These bodies are often the labour of months or years and are then handed down as heirlooms. The skirt is dark coloured and always of different material from the body. It is usually in two parts; the upper being of striped material, the rest of dark blue with a band of reddish brown at the bottom. The sleeves are in two parts. From the wrist to just above the elbow, they are usually of dark blue cloth; from the shoulder to the elbow with stripes of black and white or red and white running along the length'.

The sleeves thus described are, in fact, oversleeves, drawn on to the forearm over the striped sleeves which are attached to a white body garment and are still sometimes worn. Maaskamp shows them worn directly over the white sleeves of the chemise without the striped sleeves. The jacket, basically red in colour nowadays, is usually worn over the embroidered boned bodice. The engravings chosen by Lovett show the chintz bib, pinned over the jacket as today but somewhat larger then than now. The famous cap is composed of twelve separate items, including a cardboard shape, pinned together by up to eighty pins. Today it is often replaced, even by older women, by the children's cap—a little stitched bonnet all ready to put on.

The habit of dressing little boys up to the age of five in skirts is interesting. There was in fact no danger of the knowledgeable mistaking one sex for the other as there were several specific differences in the garments of the two.

In the Volendam dress of today the most remarkable item is the winged cap or *hul,* of white lace and embroidery, worn only on special occasions over the black conical everyday cap. The angle, shape and proportion of the *hul,* as seen today, is very recent and shows a remarkable degree of development, even since one's own admittedly distant childhood. Formerly, it fitted more closely to the head and more vertically so that the smaller wings were lower down and farther apart. In its early form, in fact, it was capable of having a woollen cap worn on top, or even a bonnet. The new development is bringing about its own demise for the *hul* is now so expensive, fragile and inconvenient to wear.

For everyday in Volendam a long-sleeved purple jacket and black skirt is chosen, but the festive dress has a square necked, short sleeved jacket. The neckline is filled in with a double bib, back and front, made of glazed cotton, the pattern of which is repeated on the top section of the apron. A small neckerchief is also worn with the ends tucked into the neckline at the front. The coral necklace, as worn for best, is a double row with a large square clasp at the front.

Another style survives into current use at Bunschoten and Spakenburg, once also on the Zuyder Zee. This style not only survives but has developed into a remarkably eccentric fashion with little regard for

87 A Friesland lady of the nineteenth century (1887). The neck-frill of the headdress later became shorter, as it can still be seen when revived for festive occasions.

96

Norwegian Lapps. 19th century
Lappen aus Norwegen. 19. Jahrhundert
Lapon et Laponne de Norvège. XIXᵉ siècle

Denmark. North Falster. Mid 19th century
Dänemark. Nord Falster. Mitte des 19. Jahrhunderts
Danemark. Falster du nord. Milieu du XIXe siècle

Iceland. Festival dress
Island. Festtagsgewand
Islande. Costume de fête

Netherlands. Man from Volendam and young girl from Marken
Niederlande. Mann aus Volendam und Mädchen aus Marken
Pays-Bas. Jeune homme de Volendam et fillette de Marken

88 The interior of a house on Marken in the late nineteenth century.

89 The dress of Marken, from E. Maaskamp's *Representations of dresses in the Kingdom of Holland, 1811.* The basic style has survived until recent times.

convenience in wearing. Here, the double bib, as seen in Volendam and as worn elsewhere in Dutch dress, has developed into a major accessory, worn on top. Stiffened with paper and starch, the shoulders of the bib, usually boldly patterned, stand out like a sandwich board, making it impossible to wear a jacket. They are, therefore, not practical in very bad weather. Here, the headdress is a little cap of bold crochet, made at home and worn on the back of the head behind the rolled hairstyle.

At Urk, on the other hand, the double bib, though worn on top, is not stiffened, nor does it stand out from the shoulders.

The *ear-iron* has already been mentioned. This is a band of metal, gold or silver, which passes round the back or over the top of the head and to which the cap is attached. In different districts it has developed into different shapes and sizes and is worn at differing angles to affect the shape of the completed headdress.

Staphorst, on the far side of the former Zuyder Zee, is a village with a reputation for being highly religious and actively hostile to strangers, but also for its colourful houses and dress. For every day and indoors the women's headdress is a close cap of brightly patterned cloth, but the foundation of the best headdress is a black undercap over which is a broad *ear-iron.* Its upper edge, stands higher than the top of the head so that the

90 Dress in North Brabant. Bing and Von Ueberfeldt, 1857. The dress can be seen to be related to that of neighbouring Belgium. The two territories had only recently become separate.

lace cap worn over it, and only partly concealing it, is shaped into a ridge. The spiral terminals of the *ear-iron* are worn low on the cheeks. The men's attire is notable for its many large silver buttons.

The biggest of these head clasps is that formerly worn, and still revived for folk occasions though not in real life, in Friesland. It forms almost a complete cap of metal and was often worn without a covering headdress. The lace cap, when worn, fitted closely over it and other gold ornaments and pins were worn at the forehead. This lace cap, which in the nineteenth century had a long curtain-like veil in the neck, became shorter at a later date, and as now revived the neck veil is vestigial. Similar caps which also modified their size and style were once worn in neighbouring localities and right down the North Sea coast, for instance at Katwijk.

The area with the most variety of styles is Zeeland. South of Rotterdam, the headdress with the flowing veil has increased its fullness, contrary to the situation in the north. There are so many other styles the most interesting being that of South Beveland where the two religions, Catholic and Protestant, produce two related but differing fashions, particularly in the headdress and the decoration of the bodice. The Protestant headdress spreads wide in an oval shape, whereas the Catholic version is angular. In both styles the decorations of the *ear-iron* are rectangular plaques. The Protestants wear these on the temples with the hair rolled between, but the Catholics wear them close together at the top of the forehead, there being no roll of hair.

In the Land of Axel, near the Belgian border, we find a style of great individuality. The headdress is a small lace cap, under which the hair is worn in two loops at the front and with gold spirals near the top of the forehead. The main interest, however, is centred on the neckerchief, dark patterned and silken and the size of a shawl. Elsewhere, the neckerchief is often folded and pinned down at the back to reveal the back of the neck. In Axel, it is drawn right down to the waist and anchored with a large safety pin, padded on the shoulders to ear level with paper. At both front and back, the heavily beaded sleeveless top bodice is thus revealed,

91 A Volendam interior according to Bing and Von Ueberfeldt, 1857. The old form of the *hul* is shown.

99

framed by the folds of the shawl.

In the other southern provinces, in Limburg and North Brabant, what surviving dress there is is of a different character, more urban in style and with few special characteristics remaining, apart from the caps. Caps, in fact, are what characterize a number of regions in the Netherlands, where the rest of the attire has lost any folk elements it ever had. In some cases, of course, the styles were always based on recent burgher fashions. Although caps, as we have seen, have tended to enlarge and elaborate themselves, this very tendency brings its own difficulties when the wearer can no longer put the headdress on for herself nor even launder and set it without professional help. When such help is no longer available the style is doomed to extinction.

Belgium and Luxemburg

92 Luxemburg. Costume for a folk-dance group.

It is strange to find a country in Europe with no real tradition of regional dress, especially when it is adjacent to a country with a strong tradition, with which it shares a language and with which, less than a hundred and fifty years ago, it was united. Yet this is the situation we find when we move on from the Netherlands to Belgium.

Whereas the end of the eighteenth century saw the development of regional styles almost everywhere else, there was apparently no romantic age in Belgium. The countries with the strongest traditions of folk dress are often those with well developed folk arts. It is perhaps significant that these were not well developed either.

This is not to say that there were no class distinctions in dress, no peasant dress or dress of the working townspeople. Naturally there were, just as there were, for instance, in England but, as in England, there was no distinction between localities. There was no organized opinion about what it was proper for people to wear as festive dress, in fact, no feeling for *our dress* at all. Since the people were not 'discovered' there is little relevant literature or illustrative material which, whether it be cause or effect, only appears when there is something to encourage or record.

The main items by Jean-Baptiste Madou: *Costumes belgiques,* 1830, and *Collection des provinces de la Belgique,* 1835, have between them a large number of coloured plates but they show, not regional dress or even a consistent style for the whole country, but occupational dresses: milk

93 A lacemaker, from *Collection des provinces de la Belgique* by J. B. Madou, 1835.

girls, laundresses, lace-makers, mostly urban workers. Dress shown other than work clothes seems to belong to ordinary town fashions. We have seen something of this in the dress of the southern Netherlands in North Brabant, once part of an extended Flanders, and Limburg, where the caps, though large and elaborate, have a style less developed towards local individuality. They are bourgeois in type. If there is an item which characterizes the dress of nineteenth century Belgium it is the cap, very much in the same style as in the neighbouring provinces. The Sunday fashions of the people then were those of the bourgeoisie.

Perhaps the reason is that the occupations of the people in this closely populated land were service occupations and the provision of food to the towns, to which they looked also as the centres of their own culture. (This does not explain why in the Netherlands strong traditions of local dress often persist on the outskirts of large towns as at Scheveningen near the Hague, why the fishmarket women coming in to Copenhagen were among the last surviving examples of local dress in real life in Denmark and why one of the few remaining examples in Yugoslavia is the dress of the Konavle valley adjacent to Dubrovnik and is still to be seen in the markets there.)

Because of the history of the Duchy of Luxemburg there has never been a specifically Luxemburger dress. Just as Belgium was once part of a greater Flanders which included North Brabant, Flemish Zeeland and northern France, the present Grand Duchy of Luxemburg was once part of a duchy four times its present size, and, what is more, a political reality until it lost territory to Prussia and Belgium. The history of its dress, then, is part of the history of its component parts. One can find material on the Eifel and Saarland, once part of the Duchy, but the present Grand Duchy is no more rewarding on this matter than Belgium. Here again, the cap, with full crown and long gathered front was much worn, but that is the only item which could be remarked on. However, this has not prevented the folk dance societies of the present day from producing a costume in which to perform. Generally the boys wear blue smocks and the girls a dress and apron of rural type and a cap with lappets.

104

Germany

94 Bavaria. Lower Franconia. A bride and bridegroom from Ochsenfurt, 1920. The bride's headdress would be replaced by a conical hood like that in no. 99.

The styles which are best known and which for most people seem to characterize the German folk dress are those of Upper Bavaria. This is not surprizing for, as already mentioned, the revival in the nineteenth century and much of the survival of the dress stem from the enthusiasm of royal and aristocratic patrons, there and in neighbouring Austria. Also from 1883, when the first one was founded, the societies for the preservation of costume, the *Trachtenvereine,* were active in this area, basing their regulation patterns upon the hunting dress of the men and those for the women on styles which were still in use and which continue to survive. Consequently, the wearing of folk dress is not confined to organized groups, though no doubt it eventually will be. There are, because of the concern and interest in preserving the local customs, a few areas where the traditional dress is still worn for festivals and even on Sundays for instance, in the areas of Miesbach and the valley of the Isar, whereas before the last war it was worn generally.

While the traditional dress was developing, up to the nineteenth century, Germany was not united as a nation. Even the sumptuary laws which delayed their early growth were the edicts of different governments and, consequently, the picture is a complicated one which cannot be adequately described in a small space. There are, however, a number of common elements, not just as the result of the revival movement, which tends to unify the styles, but genuine Germanic ingredients in the dress which derive from earlier times. The paintings of Dürer and Cranach are not without relevance to the basic shape of the female dress. If we add further elements, especially from the eighteenth and nineteenth centuries, like the closed jacket or *Spenzer* we have the alternative style to the *Mieder* or laced bodice. Versions of these appear throughout Germany. Earlier the laced bodice was an undress working style and only later became adopted as formal wear or festival wear for the young. Even then rules of etiquette often forbade its appearance in church. The closed jacket, originally worn over the bodice, eventually tended to replace it or be worn on different occasions. In the region of Miesbach, for example, while young women wear the *Mieder* as festival dress; the older women who would wear the high-necked *Spenzer* ordinarily, have a special kind, the *Schalk,* for festival wear made of black silk with ruched upper sleeves and more ruching round the low neck which is often filled with flowers. The typical hat today is the shallow conical *Spitzhut,* plain or with rows of cord round the crown, ending at the back in two tassels. Formerly, green hats like those of the men were worn.

In Upper and Old Bavaria at Werdenfels and Friedberg, in Austria in Kleines Walsertal and elsewhere in Vorarlberg, fur caps are worn by women, not for warmth but for best. They have developed, it appears, from fur-edged undercaps or indoor caps and in old prints they may be seen worn with large hats on top.

Partly in Bavaria and partly in Baden-Würtemberg is Swabia, no longer a political entity, but a convenient division for our purpose and indeed a living cultural entity for its people. Lying as it does in the vicinity of Lake Constance, adjacent to the Swiss and Austrian borders and merging into the Black Forest area beyond which lies France, it will be realized how significant this corner of Germany is for its folk dress and for the influences given to and taken from its neighbours.

The striking feature of the dress of Swabia is the variety of headdresses, in particular the variants of the *Radhaube,* or wheel-shaped cap. This appears to be a particularly vigorous development of the caps deriving from the fashionable French hood of the Renaissance, which in several of its manifestations has a tendency to rise and flatten behind, especially in its German versions. In some versions it is worn hat-like, that is shading the brows, in others like a halo, standing away from the head on a small foundation. The materials vary also. It may be of chenille trimmed with gold lace, or even entirely golden. The style, however, is not confined to Germany. Versions are met with from middle Franconia, through Swabia and Austria in the region of Lake Constance; on the Swiss side also, for instance at St. Gallen.

95 Lusatia. Sponsor and bridesmaid at a wedding in Bluno. Contemporary.

96 Black Forest. Girl from the Gutach Valley. Sunday dress still worn today.

97 Lusatia. Girl from Cunersdorf, (Lower Lusatia), in Sunday dress.

The Black Forest and the Rhine area really demands a book to itself. This area of Germany has kept a varied selection of folkdress in active use more than any other. The Gutachtal, for instance, still uses its Sunday dress with the remarkable straw hat trimmed with eleven woollen balls—red for unmarried girls, black for matrons, worn over a black cap with a stiff veil shading the eyes. The dress to go with it consists of a black velvet bodice embroidered with sprigs of flowers and a stiff brocade apron over a black pleated skirt, under which is worn a red petticoat. The marital status of the men in Gutachal is also marked by the hatstyle and colour of the waistcoat.

In the mountain area near Triberg is a group of villages where the women wear top hats in bright colours—yellow in the vicinity of Schonach, orange in the Prechtal and scarlet in the Elztal. Here, in the central Black Forest region the tendency is to wear the *halsmantel*, a kind of collar which fills in the neckline, just as one sees in many of the dresses of Switzerland and the Tyrol.

Hanauerland, (nothing to do with the town of Hanau near Frankfurt) is the area between the Forest and the Rhine on the other side of which is French Alsace. The dress of the two regions is closely related. The female headdress consists of variations, large and small, of the bow, supposedly tying a cap, but usually overwhelming it completely.

In the upper Black Forest, we find a fashion in black silk, rather conical caps, *Backenhaube*, with embroidered tops to the crowns, decorated and tied on with broad, black, picot-edged ribbons. These, apart from the embroidery, seem to be related to a form of headdress found with variations of angle and size over a wide area of Germany. The chaplet of flowers or beads worn tied on top of the head by young girls and brides is also found widely distributed from Lower Franconia through Swabia to the Rhineland and Switzerland.

If we, in fact, return to the northern part of Bavaria, Lower Franconia, we see something of a break from the alpine tradition of dress thought of as typically Bavarian, to a style transitional with that of Hesse and northern Germany. In Lower Franconia, in the region of Ochsenfurt, the remnants of the dress still survive worn by extremely old ladies for church going, though the typical high shoulders are no longer part of the style. The full dress is worn, of course, in revived form by folk dance groups. The dress, inherited by a friend of the author, from her godmother who was married in it about 1920, is typical. The black closely pleated skirt with a narrow red edge comes not quite to the ankle. The apron, richly patterned with flowers has a broad zig-zag ribbon across it. The jacket, with *gigot* sleeves, has a low square neck, leaving a broad band below on each side which wraps over in double breasted style and is heavily embroidered with braid and sequins. The opening is filled with a fringed scarf, pulled well through. The cuffs are embroidered like the lower bodice, almost to the elbow. Fingerless knitted or beaded mittens should be worn. The bride's chaplet would be replaced by a conical black silk headdress with broad ribbons behind. The hairstyle, in which complicated braids are arranged like a bow, is still worn by old women who can get the necessary assistance. Since the war, however, the head has been covered by an ordinary scarf. Similarly, the fine silver jewelry is now rare, most of it sold during the war.

In Hesse the active wearing of folk dress did not last quite so long. By 1870 it had been abandoned by the men, but women were wearing it, though less and less, for the first twenty-five years of this century. Fortunately, a live interest was revived just in time, starting, for instance, at Schlitz in south Hesse near Fulda, in 1926, with what was to be a series of folk dress festivals. These were revived after the Second World War, attracting groups from all over Hesse, elsewhere in Germany and eventually from abroad. The interest continues and the work is being furthered by a newly founded Local History Society. The dress of Schlitz is somewhat transitional between the styles of south Germany and those to the northwest in that the chaplet and a smaller version of the black silk *Haube* are featured as well as a tendency for the skirts to be shorter.

In northern Hesse, near Marburg, we find that the *Haube* has become pill-box sized and, in the nearby area of the Schwalm, it merely serves to contain the knot of hair which is entirely swept on top. Ribbons floating behind take away a little of the severity. The skirts are unusually short and, as between ten and fourteen of them were worn together and, in the old dress, though not as revived, a very high, stiff, busk-like plastron was tucked into the bodice strings, the dress presented a somewhat squat and bulky line. Girls wore red, young women green, older women lilac and the elderly assumed black dresses. Etiquette was also strict; the dress of communicants with its high stiff veil worn with a black dress was like deep mourning. There was no question of men appearing except for work, in undress waistcoated style. There were even strict occasions when the blue jacket rather than the white coat might be worn. The wedding attire for both bride and groom was overwhelming in the elaboration of its decoration.

In the north east, in Schaumberg-Lippe, we have another example of a dress which was encouraged by noble patronage, and which, consequently, has survived to recent times. Not only has it survived but has done so in elaborate style. We see the chaplet used as bridal wear, but here it is uncommonly large and high. At Lindhorst neck frills are very characteristic, and so is the conical black silk *Haube,* worn far forward and tied under the chin as well as draped behind.

In the north, near Hamburg, the dress of Vierlande is unmistakable because of its wide hat of strange shape worn over a cap with a flat bow behind. The women were often to be seen in Hamburg market. They wore a brownish red skirt trimmed with green or black and pleated closely at the top. The decorative plastron or bib was high and square, but not stiff. The jacket was, for weekdays, of blue or green sprigged cotton but for Sundays was of cloth matching the skirt, the bib showing through an almost circular opening. Long plaits were worn even by older women. The men's dress was very fine, including a blue or red waistcoat with two rows of silver buttons, plush fall-front breeches trimmed with purple and with large buttons below the waist. On weekdays the jacket was merely waist length, whereas on Sundays it was longer with two vents, and was worn with a top hat.

In Lusatia (Lausitz), for centuries a Slavic enclave in one or other of the German Lands and now in East Germany, we have an extremely interesting example of surviving folk dress. Everyday dress and to some extent, Sunday dress is still worn by old women, but even ten years ago the special festive costumes were rare. The ordinary dress makes much use of blue, i.e. indigo printed materials for both skirts and spenser tops and other plain or printed materials, sometimes very bright in colour, are also used. Different areas have their own traditions and these can best be seen

98 Schaumburg-Lippe. Festival dress from Lindhorst. Middle of the twentieth century.

99 Bavaria. Lower Franconia. Woman from Röttingen. Lithograph by Peter Geist, 1852.

100 Swabia. The Allgäu. (Neighbourhood of Kempten.) *c.* 1845.

in the festive dresses, of which we might look at two examples. In central Lusatia, around Hoyerswerda, we see a costume of astonishing richness of decoration worn for weddings, yet upon examination, the effect is obtained by economical means as far as outlay is concerned, though requiring much work, for the area has always been rather poor. The main parts of the dress are white, embroidered over large areas in eyelet and white embroidery, with special styling of the sleeves. The entire front of the bodice is covered with a plastron of brightly coloured glass beads; it can, of course be handed down, and its materials are showy rather than expensive. There is, for instance, no fine silver or precious jewelry as in more prosperous areas. In Lower Lusatia, one's attention is immediately drawn to the large folded white headdress, nowadays put on complete rather than dressed on the head. The wide, standing pleated collars which stand up behind the head like sixteenth century ruffs are also a feature.

101 Woman from Vierlande in Hamburg market. End of the nineteenth century.

102 Hanauer Land. R. Gleichauf, 1860.

103 Central Black Forest. Painting by Rudolf Gleichauf, 1860.

110

Austria

The modern Republic of Austria consists of eight provinces plus Vienna: Upper Austria, Lower Austria, Salzburg, Styria, Tyrol, Vorarlberg, Carinthia and Burgenland. With the loss of the empire the country contains a fairly homogeneous nation but there are minorities in the borderlands: Croats and Magyars in Burgenland and Slovenes in Carinthia.

The provinces occupy a compact area except for the Tyrol and Vorarlberg which extend to the west between Germany, Switzerland and Italy, a situation which has an effect on the folk dress. Each province has its historical folk dress and has enthusiastically kept it alive, revived and renewed for festive wear. All the provinces have their literature. Local societies publish patterns and they can also be bought in shops, some of the latter being patterns adapted for party wear. In resorts like Salzburg,

104 Revived town dress. Salzkammergut.

as in Germany at Nürnberg or Munich, such garments may be bought in expensive *Tracht* shops at select prices. The popularity of the simplified *Dirndl* style and the tailored suit has tended to put the older more elaborate styles into the background, except for members of organized groups, but in many areas the revived styles retain their traditional form.

The most westerly and smallest of the provinces is Vorarlberg. At its north west extremity it touches Lake Constance at the town of Bregenz. It is not surprizing, therefore, that the styles to be found in the area are much like those of neighbouring Germany and Switzerland. In particular, the *wheel-cap* of Swabia is typical here also. The costume societies have revived for the town of Bregenz itself, an urban style consisting of a silk dress in the *Biedermeier* manner to go with a gold *radhaube*. Most towns in Austria have kept alive such a style for festive occasions worn with the cap appropriate to the district. The men, likewise have a nineteenth century frock coat and breeches. Away from the towns the fashion is different and, in fact, specially worth noticing. A small valley, Kleines Walsertal, on the German border, and only easily accessible on the German side, preserves a dress rather unlike the others of Swabia, although the typical fur cap appears to have come from there. The women's dress is high waisted, hanging from a short bodice, and apparently a successor to a simple smock dress of an earlier age, without the adoption of a laced bodice. The apron is also worn high and the sleeved jacket is extremely short. This is one of the localities where a fur cap is worn by women for best. The dress of the Bregenz Forest area is not unlike that of Kleines Walsertal, in that the dress called *Juppo* hangs from

105 Dress of the Carinthian-Yugoslav border at the beginning of the twentieth century.

106 Women from Pinzgau in Salzburger Land.

112

embroidered shoulder straps. The garment itself is of glazed black linen in close pleats. Here, however, the apron is tied round at the natural waistline and the accompanying jacket is longer. Young girls wear a small crown, seen elsewhere in the territory of Swabian influence, like a basket, or the framework of the beaded or flowered chaplet so widely worn. The normal headdress is the *Spitzkappe*, a conical, mushroom-shaped woolly hat, called also *Blaukappe* for its blue colour and in the Tyrol called *Fazzelkappe*. Though somewhat unbecoming, it was evidently worn from an early date in many localities throughout the Tyrol and Vorarlberg. A hat could be worn over it.

Elsewhere in Vorarlberg and through the Tyrol, indeed through much of Austria, the style is a basic one of skirt, laced bodice with coloured plastron, a collar covering the throat and shoulders, here called *Goller*, or a kerchief. Again, young women may wear the small chaplet, but in the

107 Girls from Lungau in Salzburger Land. Revived dress.

Tyrol a wide, curly brimmed hat, covered or edged and banded with green silk is the proper wear in many districts. The oldest ones are the widest. In fact, hat sizes tend to shrink as the dress develops. In the revived dress the green trimmed hats are worn, especially in the middle Inn valley near Innsbruck, to the south and in the Wipptal. To the north and in Innsbruck itself, black hats have always been traditional.

Most inconveniently for the arrangement of this book, the territory beyond the Brenner Pass has, since the First World War, belonged to Italy. The people are still German speaking, however, and the folk dress cannot be separated from that of North and East Tyrol, which remain in Austria. Moreover, the area near Merano (Meran) and the Val Venosta (Vintschgau) was not only the seat of the old rulers and Earl Marshalls of the Tyrol, but is also the area from which the essential spirit of the Tyrolean dress springs and which contains probably its best examples. It was here that the short breeches revealing the knee originated. Austrian books on the dress of the Tyrol tend to ignore the political boundary and treat the area as a whole. However, the political reality is now sixty years old and unlikely to alter so we must return to northern Italy later. Still within the Austrian border is the Ötztal where the old dress was most picturesque. The man wore short black breeches above the knee and often, footless white socks. The braces were red, over a white shirt. The short jacket, without lapels, was embroidered on the front edges and cuffs. The woman had a black skirt and blue apron. Her chemise had a lace edged collar over which a bright scarf was crossed. The purplish bodice was laced with gold strings and behind the lacing was tucked a large stiff stomacher with gold embroidery. She also wore footless stockings and the hats of both man and woman were wide-brimmed and rather low in the crown. The revived dress is much like that of neighbouring areas on the south of the upper Inn valley. In the Zillertal there was formerly a hat for both men and women, with a high slender crown of great elegance and with gold tassels at the front. The latter have been kept but they now adorn the somewhat bulbous conical hat of the newer style.

The provinces of Upper Austria, Salzburg and Styria (Steiermark) occupy the centre of the country and contain the beautiful area of the Salzkammergut. Upper Austria is the source of certain influential elements in the folk dress, particularly of the other central provinces. Thus the *Dirndl* is the development of the working dress of the Salzkammergut, centred on Bad Ischl. The gold caps, much worn by urban citizens, are often developments of or influenced by those of Linz. The hats of the country women have wide turned down brims with small crowns with ribbons to tie them on.

The main contribution of Styria to Austrian folk dress is the grey or green loden jacket which is influential throughout the Alpine region. The version known as the *Haftel* is a long jacket like an eighteenth century collarless coat, with contrasting neck facing and cuffs. Many of the jackets of Styria make use of such contrasts. An embroidered waistcoat with knob-shaped silver buttons and cord loops may be worn under the *Haftel*. Trousers are leather, rather full, and fasten below the knee.

In the lower Inn Valley, stretching into Upper Bavaria and most particularly in the province of Salzburg, we find a hat style with a low, black, boater-like crown, decorated with gold cords and worn with a low-necked spenser and black skirt with a contrasting long light apron. The hat is tied on behind with long wide ribbons reaching to the hem. Again, it

114

108 Tyrol. Innsbruck region. B. de Moleville, 1804. Both the wide-brimmed hat and the conical *Fazzel kappe* remained typical during the nineteenth century.

109 Tyrol. Ötztal, by Alois Kirchebner, 1840s.

appears that the older style of hat was taller. The man's dress is characterized by knee breeches of black leather with elaborate white embroidery, worn with a green or brown jacket.

In Lower Austria we find a great many varieties of closed sleeveless bodices, often worn nowadays with matching skirts, as are the various sleeved spensers. The variety of caps is very great in this province also. As well as the adopted gold cap from Linz there are others, for instance, that of Wachau, also gold but retaining a bonnet shape, the crown pleated on and pinched out like a fan behind. The dress of the men is also well developed in this province with embroidered and patterned waistcoats in many styles including the *brustfleck,* a waistcoat with no front opening but crossed behind with strings and tied in front, a style developed from a bib-like false front. There is an equally large variety of jackets.

In contrast the dress of Carinthia, (Kärnten) seems antique, having developed less from its early traditional style. The old German fashion of wearing undercaps under the wide hat for instance might be seen in Carinthia until a late date. The province is comparatively undeveloped with industry so that agriculture, the timber trade and livestock engage the people and the dress is, therefore, of an occupational character. There is, nevertheless, some development of style and it shows the influence of neighbouring countries. The headdress worn by women where hats are not worn is usually a fringed kerchief knotted behind and this softer detail

115

is echoed in the tendency to add ribbons and fringed decorations elsewhere to the dress. Though rather stiff pleated skirts and aprons are frequent, one finds attractive plastrons covering the front of the blouse or, as in the Gail valley, a fringed scarf with a corner pinned at the throat and the other corners tied behind at the waist. The blouses have wide collars with pleated edges, often hanging well down behind. In the Carnic Alps, forming the Yugoslav border, there is a traditional style with a beautiful halo cap, now to be seen more often as a festival dress in northern Yugoslavia.

The Burgenland occupies the area south of Vienna, along the Hungarian border, and has formerly been Hungarian territory, now kept back within the new republic. It shows the characteristics of such an area and the Croatian and Magyar minorities with their own styles of architecture and dress maintain their traditions, or indeed import new ones of a 'national' character.

111 Girl from the Gailtal. Revived dress. The scarf pinned across the chest is typical of this valley.

Switzerland

112 Revived dress of the present day. Woman from the Engadine.

The folk dress of Switzerland was at its height, as in most countries of western Europe between about 1780 and 1850, after which its use declined quite rapidly with improvements in communications and in living conditions. It survived in the remotest areas, for instance in the highlands of the Valais, until modern times and as a rule, Catholic districts kept their dress longer than Protestant districts.

Fortunately, as in neighbouring Germany and Austria, there were at the end of the century people anxious to preserve the old traditions. Luckily, many of the garments were preserved in the chests of the villagers and in museums where there was also a rich archive of graphic material. Sigismund Freudenberger, a painter trained in Paris, from the 1770s onwards painted the people in the neighbourhood of Berne. Gabriel-Louis Lory and his son Mathias were also famous among many painters and engravers of the early nineteenth century. There is a collection of drawings and watercolours supported by detailed sketches by Georg-Ludwig Vogel, 1788–1879, in the Swiss National Museum which are of particular value for their accurate record of the Swiss folk dress of his time.

The revived dresses were taken from original models adapted to suitable modern materials and so preserve, more or less, the spirit of the nineteenth century illustrations from which those quite lost were reconstructed.

The traditional styles of Switzerland were influenced, as might be

113 1) and 3) Fribourg (French). 2) Schaffhausen. 4) Valais. 5) Berne. Lanté, 1827.

expected in so central and small a country, by the dress of neighbouring areas. The original cantons of the Confederation, Schwyz, Uri and Unterwald, though centrally positioned, were on the trade route to Italy and the tendency of much Swiss dress to favour rich materials and, in some cases, styles which clearly go back to the renaissance is owed to this. The cantons to the north, for instance, Basle and Schaffhausen have obvious affinities with the styles of the Rhine valley and the neighbouring parts of Germany. On the west, for instance, near Neuchâtel and Geneva we see French alpine styles. Moreover, within the country the difference between styles is not closely connected with the separate cantons, or even particular localities, so much as with geographical divisions and the lines of communication between them.

To come to the styles themselves, no doubt the butterfly-shaped headdresses worn in a number of localities are thought of as typical, especially that of Appenzell. The varieties of headdress are numerous though, ranging from a small *haube* with ribbons at Schaffhausen to extremely large straw hats, found rather generally in the French speaking areas. There was formerly a tradition for young girls to wear black headdresses and for white to be worn by married women. Remnants of this tradition may be seen in the revived dress.

During the nineteenth century there had been a tendency for formerly brightly coloured costumes to be replaced by darker ones and for ribbons and coloured decoration to be discarded in favour of silver ornaments and

114 1) Berne. 2) and 6) Appenzell. 3) Fribourg (German) 4) Lucerne. 5) Schwyz. Racinet 1888.

1   2   3   4   5

chains. In Appenzell, by the First World War, the dress had become entirely black. The revived dress restored some of the bright colours yet kept much of the silver ornament in addition.

If we take Appenzell as our first example we find, both traditionally and in the revived dress, a difference between the styles of the Protestant and Catholic areas, the Catholics wearing a much more elaborate ensemble. A long sleeved jacket, which may now be in any colour, matches the long tightly pleated skirt over which is an ample silk apron. The jacket opening is laced with chains over a plastron embroidered in gold. A somewhat square double collar, white over black with a double frill making large epaulettes, leaves the neckline open to display silver necklaces. The famous headdress of tulle is black based on a small cap of gold lace, with a second, white one worn between the wings of the first and pulled forward, in the case of married women. The Protestant dress, though employing shot taffeta for its large apron and the small part of the plastron which shows through the bodice opening is, though rich, somewhat plain with a fichu of black tulle and a small black cap with little wings of black tulle veiling the cheeks.

Schwyz also has an elaborate silken dress with a winged headdress. Here the dress is Italian in inspiration with separate sleeves laced to the bodice and pleated white frills from the elbows. The lace headdress in two upright frills was traditionally black for girls and white for matrons, while the wives of important citizens added a decoration of roses between the wings—hence the name, *Rosehube*.

The old costumes of Unterwalden, particularly that of Nidwald, were,

115 Unterwald. Hairstyle of Nidwald. Drawing by L. Vogel.

116 Unterwald (Obwald). Women of Beckenried. L. Vogel 1814.

while keeping to a peasant rather than an urban style, very rich and interesting. The large straw hats, which in Obwald were lined with flowered material, were worn over a coiffure made up with the aid of ribbons. In Obwald these were white for girls while older women used red wool, but in Nidwald a complete false chignon was made in red and worn on the back of the head pierced through with a large arrow-shaped pin. A great deal of jewelry and decoration was worn. Today, the front opening of the bodice is covered with an embroidered plastron. The neckline is filled in and round the throat there is a choker of gold and filigree plaques alternating with garnet or coral beads. In addition, a chain with pendants of silver flowers or hearts is worn. The ample sleeves are arranged in concertina pleats.

It may be observed that the headdress of Appenzell, based on a gold

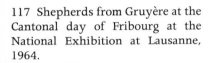

117 Shepherds from Gruyère at the Cantonal day of Fribourg at the National Exhibition at Lausanne, 1964.

121

cap, is a variant of the gold caps and 'wheel' headdresses seen in German Swabia, across the border. Actual examples of the wheel shape are also found in Switzerland. A gold one at St. Gallen, for instance, is very large, while at Zurich there is a 'plate' headdress of black satin.

Berne contains a number of interesting and original styles. Generally, in the north-east, the skirts throughout the nineteenth century were shorter than elsewhere. At Guggisberg they were very short so that the knees were bare. The skirt and bodice, joined together were black. The bodice front, in the form of a bib, was attached to the little square collar with ties at the corner or, in the absence of it, was tied round the neck. Now the dress is much the same, decorated with red on the black. The green apron, tightly gathered at the top, is buttoned to the skirt at the sides with a vertical row of three buttons. White stockings with red clocks are the correct wear and the girls have a tiny pillbox cap with ribbons in black, a style to be found also in Schaffhausen. The dress of Seeland with the blue skirt and red border, red bodice with stiff plastron in yellow, trimmed and laced in black, is that painted most often by Freudenberger and has been faithfully revived. The dress of the outskirts of Berne, with black skirt and bodice is very familiar. It provides another example of the winged headdress, this time of horsehair mesh.

In Fribourg, a similar dress to the black one from Berne is found, except that a fringed scarf is worn instead of a collar. In fact the dresses are varied in Fribourg which is a canton divided by language as well as customs.

In the south of Switzerland, Valais preserved, in the high and inaccessible valleys, its traditions of folk dress longer than anywhere else. Roads were few and modern outside influences had little effect until well into the twentieth century. Not only was the folk dress habitually worn, it was also homespun and woven in very conservative colours, mostly dark brown or black. These are made into styles of some severity, relieved by smart contrasting bands and by scarves and aprons of bought bright silk. In the valley of the Rhone, however, there are matching silk ensembles in an early nineteenth century style with the tops of the jacket sleeves gauged in tiny pleats. The accompanying hat with its rather tall crown owes its height to the vertically pleated ribbons which surround it. Formerly in more general use, but tending to disappear, was a hat with many yards of folded black ribbon sewn down to make a sort of pleated brim.

In the south east, Tessin (Ticino) not only has its styles influenced by neighbouring Italy but shares a fashion with Lombardy. The dress of Mendrisiotto has detachable sleeves tied on at the shoulder and a long pointed corsage in the Italian style. Round the back of the head arranged like a halo are some two dozen headed pins thrust into the chignon.

The other notable style in Tessin is that of the north where we find in Val Maggia and Val Verzasca a high waisted sleeveless smock of homespun in green or white with a red border. The apron is also worn high. A jacket also very short in the body but with long sleeves may be worn, though formerly a long coat was usual. A mob cap or a headscarf, with or without a hat, forms the headcovering. Formerly, footless stockings were worn and the feet could go bare, or be clad in wooden soled sandals.

The men's dress in Switzerland disappeared long before that of the women. Its style and progress followed that elsewhere in western Europe. From baggy trousered styles deriving from those of the Rennaissance, they progressed belatedly to styles of the eighteenth century but, as elsewhere, the old-fashioned modes were discarded in favour of up-to-date styles when visits to the town began to make them feel conspicuous. On the other hand, farmers and herdsmen have kept their occupational dress in unbroken use though evolving styles of their own, until modern times.

118 Sicily. Woman from Piano Dei Greci, Palermo. End of the nineteenth century.

Italy

The peasant dress of Italy has an extremely rich tradition, not only in quantity and breadth of distribution, but also in the costliness of materials employed for the festive dresses. It is not surprizing that the dress is varied since unification came late to Italy but, of course, there were always ties of language and culture in the Italian fashionable world and the dress does present a degree of national character. The variations belong to

119 Abruzzo. An engraving by B. Pinelli, 1809. The formalized embroidery on the ungathered apron, the tied-on sleeves and the head-covering are typical of the old folk dress of central Italy. The formality of the woman's dress is in contrast with the more utilitarian elements of the men's attire.

120 A piper from Abruzzo. Nineteenth century. The bagpiper was a familiar figure in the mountainous parts of Italy and, of course, is widely met with elsewhere in Europe.

regions and sometimes to particular districts, but there is not entire uniformity within localities as Italian dress was able to display rank, wealth and status, and also because some of the dresses were of great antiquity. There is a contrast, greater than in most countries, between the clothes worn every day and even on Sundays with the festive dresses. These were often of a completely different style and of a degree of elegance which one would not have expected peasants to afford or find appropriate. Jewelry also was elaborate and set with stones and seed pearls as well as being wrought in gold and silver in the manner of much peasant jewelry. Not only were such articles inherited, but in times of prosperity were sought for on the market, no doubt as tangible assets as well as decoration.

It appears that the fine quality of Italian dress goes back to early times for some of the sumptuary laws of the fifteenth and sixteenth centuries prescribed limitations which nevertheless allowed certain amounts of jewelry and trimmings of silk and velvet and did not, as usual, demand only the use of humble stuffs and plain colours.

It is interesting also to note the part played by superstition in the acquiring and wearing of certain types of jewelry. Amulets of all kinds were essential in a country so apprehensive of the evil eye. Materials like coral had protective powers which no one could afford to neglect. The rosary, constantly worn by devout Italians, was often large and worn like a necklace with pendant filigree medals containing appropriate images. The rosaries of Sicily were especially fine.

Today, not much of this is still to be seen. As in other countries the years since the Second World War have brought about the demise of the last generation to have been born into a living tradition so that, whereas until mid-century there were vestiges of the dress in remoter parts, the modern world has little room for it and festivals are the only occasions when it can be appropriately worn.

Having generalized so far about Italian dress, it must be said that in the extreme north the styles are influenced by those of neighbouring countries and, in the district of Bolzano, which used to be the South Tyrol, the dress of the German speaking population is entirely Austrian. Merano (Meran) at the end of Val Venosta (Vintschgau) is the centre of an area called the *Burggraferamt*, the political centre of the old County of Tyrol. The men's attire here consists of black breeches leaving the knees bare above white socks and supported both by a wide decorative belt and green braces of complicated pattern over a red shirt. The jacket is brown with wide red lapels. The hat, formerly the wide silk bound green hat typical of southern Tyrol, has been replaced by a black hat of squat conical shape. It has, however, retained the trimming of cords which denote the marital status of the wearer—red for a single man, red and green when newly married and green for a father. The woman's dress also is a fine example of the Tyrolean style with a low-cut, wide, boned bodice laced with a fine cord over a stomacher. The favoured colour for the apron is blue though other colours may be used; the skirt is of a tweed mixture of red and black. The neckerchief is crossed and the points fastened under the arms. As often in South Tyrol, the stockings are red.

On the other hand, Lombardy has lent some of her styles to Switzerland. Here, for instance, is a decoration for the hair, the *raggiera*, wherein large pins are set at the back of the head like a halo, corresponding exactly to a style employed in Tessin.

The Roman Campagna (not to be confused with Campania, the province of Naples) provides the central and typical example of Italian folk dress known to the outside world. The item of chief interest is the headdress, the *tovaglia,* of white linen folded on the head to hang down the back and often at the sides also. This and the stiff, pointed bodice are the chief elements of the dress. The *tovaglia* is not confined, however, to the region of Rome but is quite general in the Abruzzi to the east and elsewhere in the Appenines. This is not surprising for there has long been traffic and recruitment of labour in the mountains for the farmers of the plain. Besides, this headdress is centuries old and has had time to spread its influence. It is found not only as far afield as southern Dalmatia across the Adriatic but also in western Hungary.

Not only is the headdress of ancient origin, but the method of attaching sleeves to the bodice with ties, allowing the undergarment to puff out, is certainly a fashionable style from centuries ago. Such elaborations are reserved for proper occasions but the headdress belongs also to everyday and could be seen occasionally until the middle of the twentieth century.

Abruzzo, or the Abruzzi, is the name of the central Appenines east of the Roman Plain, rising up behind the town of Aquila, famous for its lace. The area is inhospitable and wild with isolated villages on hilltops and formerly very backward in development of any kind. The lives of the people were ruled by superstitions, the number of which was boundless. Yet these same conditions were productive of handicrafts and styles of folk dress and the cause of their preservation to a late date.

Many of the dresses were bright in colour, blue being a widespread favourite. At Pescocostanzo the stiff pointed bodice, the folded *tovaglia* and the tied sleeves are as typical as in the Roman Campagna. The white aprons with embroidered panels in conventional or heraldic patterns were worn tucked under the point of the bodice and bands of embroidery decorated the skirt. Near the village of Mascione brightly striped petticoats in many colours were worn under heavy darker skirts, with sleeved jackets over the bodice when going out. The *tovaglia* here hung loose and the *fasciatrella,* the coloured cloth often worn over the *tovaglia,* was usually green and hung loose also. In contrast, at Sulmona, the red cloth was narrowly folded over a white one which hung to the waist with long fringes.

The dress of Scanno is unique, not only in Abruzzo but in Italy. The blouse, with drooping, full sleeves was black and for older women, the skirt also. For younger women the skirt might be brightly coloured, but the blouse was always black. The unique item was the headdress, a complicated construction of folded scarves like a flat-topped toque, black with a broad panel of white. This was worn hat-like on top of the braided hair which was wound with white or coloured ribbon as, apparently, was the hair of women in localities where it did not show. The widows of Scanno not only wore black but draped their throats and chins also. The bride's headdress of blue and white was the only remnant of a previous style of brilliant colour and exotic details which one would not place in Italy at all; it appears to be of oriental inspiration.

In the south of Abruzzo and in Molise the old styles of dress continued the basic fashion of the Campagna but with greater richness. The typical apron was flat, often wider at the top than the bottom, and folded over for about a foot below the waist, displaying embroidered panels and borders to advantage. The dress of the men in these areas was or had become

121 Woman from Catanzaro in southern Calabria. Her dress is quite unlike the other styles to be found in Italy. Nineteenth century.

126

plainer and darker with some outbursts of colour for festive occasions. At Mascione, for instance, the traditional wedding jacket of the bridegroom matched the dress of the bride, of wool or silk in a bright colour and was worn with purple trousers. For ordinary wear the dress was utilitarian. Throughout the Campagna and the neighbouring mountains shepherds and herdsmen wore breeches with legcloths over their bright woollen stockings, their moccasin shoes tied on with straps. Black hats were decorated with flowers or feathers. Woollen cloaks, or garments of sheepskin, were proof against the weather, especially with the aid of the large cotton umbrellas beloved of peasants everywhere.

In Basilicata, or Lucania, we again find aprons with designs of heraldic animals worn over deep red or yellow skirts with velvet bodices. Ribbons tied round the neck hung down the back.

Near Brindisi in Apulia, the heel of Italy, the village of Alberobello has a unique aspect in that the dress uses no colours other than black and white to match the architecture. This is ordinary enough for everyday, but for festival wear the dress of the women includes decorated stiff wide collars of a most inconvenient size.

In Calabria, the toe of Italy, patterned silk and brocade seem to dominate some of the best known styles, for Calabria has a long-established silk industry. In Spezzano, near Cozenza, the festive dresses are made entirely of pleated silk, a product of the ribbon trade. The component parts are all attached to the tight bodice in appropriate widths of the material, skirts faced at the hem, basque and sleeves from the elbow, all tightly pleated like fans. Even the headdress is a gathered circle pulled into a point.

122 1. Cervara. 2. Sonnino. 4. Agnam. 3. and 5. 'Cociare' — Appenine types wearing moccasins. Racinet, 1888.

By contrast, at Catanzero, near the opposite coast, the spirit of the costume is entirely different, again of an exotic appearance, not only because of its colouring but its style. The cut is simple, from straight panels and the decoration emphasizes the cut. The ensemble is topped by a high-fronted crown, draped from the peak.

The men's dress of Calabria is sober apart from a taste for velveteen ribbon-edged jackets and waistcoats and splendid wide belts. The typical hat is somewhat Spanish in shape having a dished brim and a tall conical crown with pompoms or ribbons hanging from it. It was worn tilted on one side.

Sicily also has a strong tradition of folk dress both simple and formal in style. Near Taormina there is a rather simple style with a long brightly coloured plain skirt with contrasting ribbons in rows round the bottom and a small apron, often semi-circular and embroidered or made of lace, worn with a laced bodice. In other styles more elaborately patterned fabrics may be used, sometimes very rich indeed, for a dress with or without sleeves, the top often matching the skirt. Beautiful jewelry is a feature of Sicilian dress including pendant rosaries and heavy silver belts of linked plates fastened with elaborate buckles bearing devotional portraits. Also typical is a large flat rosette of embroidered ribbon on the breast.

Belgium. Man from Brussels region and milkmaid from Ostend. Early 19th century
Belgien. Mann aus Brüssel und Milchfrau aus Ostende. Frühes 19. Jahrhundert
Belgique. Habitant de la région de Bruxelles et laitière d'Ostende. Début du XIXe siécle

German couple from Eastern Pomerania. 19th century
Paar aus dem ehemals deutschen Pommern. 19. Jahrhundert
Couple allemand de Poméranie de l'est. XIXe siècle

Austria. Young woman with man from Salzburg region. 1900

Österreich. Junge Frau und älterer Mann aus dem Salzburger Land. 1900

Autriche. Jeune femme et vieil homme de la région de Salzbourg. 1900

France. Peasants from Eaux Bonnes, Pyrenees. c.1830
Frankreich. Paar aus Eaux Bonnes, Pyrenäen. ca.1830
France. Paysan et paysanne d'Eaux Bonnes, Pyrénées. Environ 1830

France

France occupies a unique position in Europe. Its large size and extreme westerly position, the long seabord, the land borders relatively stable once unification was established at an early date—these factors are contributory to the nature of French social development. The personal character of the French people is another important factor.

The old courts of Burgundy and France were centres of fashion, both receptive and influential. Worldly tastes were established here; they were the arbiters. In modern unified France, Paris has always been the centre of affairs. This, one might think, would not affect the lives of the peasantry who have always formed the greater part of the population. Under the control of the landowners they lived their hard lives in their own localities. Yet they were affected also, since the local influences on what they wore came from a central source. Their clothing had not been truly primitive, in the eastern European sense, for centuries; they were playing their part in the evolution of Western European fashion. The more remote the area was from Paris, the more backward were its peasant fashions. Occupations like fishing and seagoing gave a different basic style to the workclothes of the men than did agriculture. The sumptuary laws held back the development of rural fashions. But a certain worldliness in the French character meant that they would accept gladly any chance to improve their style of dress, if necessary in defiance of the law. By the time of the Revolution some move forward in the conditions of the people was discernible and was beginning to be reflected in their dress.

There was not, however, the incentive in most of France to promote a national culture in defiance of foreign rule as in Bohemia, or even Norway. (Brittany, Alsace and the Basques are a separate case.) On the other hand, the Romantic Age came to France too, and the peasantry were 'discovered' by artists and writers here as they were elsewhere. So in the middle of the nineteenth century there was an increased development of interest in regional styles which established themselves firmly enough to last and evolve for several generations; in some conservative areas, to recent times. The romantic influences fell on fertile ground. Credit must be given to the people themselves for the considerable artistry of their dress, but the basic style from which the development evolved depended on the stage which had been reached in the area at the time of this post-revolutionary surge forward. In backward areas like Brittany it was pre-Revolutionary; elsewhere, for instance in Bourbonnais, the styles were more contemporary. In much of France, then, the influence of the fashionable world was strong and the urban fashions of the nineteenth century are the main sources. The coincidental growth of the French textile industry, making a wide range of fabrics generally available for the first time, as well as the spread of fashion literature, provided the people with the materials and patterns they needed.

130

123 Brittany. Young couple from Plougastel-Daoulas (Finistère) in the twentieth century revived dress. 1950s.

124 Coiffe of Pont l'Abbé (Finistère), 1928. This is the well known coiffe *bigouden*, which has since doubled its height.

What marks the main difference in the French regional styles is the headdress of the women. Some are modest and conservative, some match those of the Netherlands both in their enterprising shape and form and their ability to develop in most unpromising conditions, both social and climatic. Why the fish-sellers of the Channel ports should have developed such elaborate starched headdresses or, for that matter, how the enormous confections worn in Normandy survived the weather is a mystery. Why in the Ile d'Oléron in the Bay of Biscay, the headdresses should be equally elaborate and why the coiffes of Brittany should still be increasing in size in an area as inclement as the Finistère peninsula is not a subject for logical speculation.

The headdresses are not only the most prominent feature of Breton dress, but they are also very numerous and varied. As always, the farther

from Paris, the more varied the dress. Britanny is not only distant but was formerly rather isolated from communication except by sea. Moreover, she is not only devoted to her local customs and strong religious faith, there is also an increasing degree of Breton as opposed to French nationalism.

By 1928 most of the headdresses had achieved their present state of development, but it is evident that almost all the apparently different shapes ultimately derive from a bonnet-shaped cap known in England as the mob cap, but of common occurrence all over Europe, which contains the hair at the back and has a front piece which folds over, sometimes extending down the side in lappets. It is these lappets which have become modified and draped or twisted to provide the shapes now current. Even the vertical caps, like the famous *Bigouden* of Pont l'Abbé and Plogastel-Saint German on the south-west coast derives from a diminished version

125 A very simple form of Breton cap from Laniscat, central Brittany. This is the kind of cap from which many of the elaborate styles have developed.

126 Pyrenees. Woman from Laruns with both skirt and leggings turned up to work in the fields. *c.* 1830.

132

127 Auvergne. Peasant women of Granetias, near Thiers. *c.* 1865. The two typical kinds of headdress—the straw bonnet over a coiffe and the linen hood are shown here.

of such a cap, tied on top of the head, since when it has grown upwards. By 1928 it was 17 cm high. Now it measures about 33 cm, which must be incommoding in a car or at the cinema. Another vertical coiffe, that of Plougastel-Daoulas, further up the coast, is severely plain and contains all the hair pulled on top. Formerly it sat further down on the head, but like many of the styles it is now worn to show more hair. Quite a different headdress is the *Cornette*, worn in a number of localities as festival wear and usually associated with the Indian shawls which have been imported into the Breton Port of Lorient since the eighteenth century. This is a large piece of stiffened lace rolled into a point and worn over the hair or over a small cap.

The dresses with which the caps are worn are not spectacular in style. Often sombre in colour, easy of fit and with rather wide sleeves from a low shoulder line, yet they each have their own beautiful accessories and embroidery of extreme refinement and taste. The men's dress has become somewhat modernized. Formerly the general wear was light-coloured baggy breeches called *braies* which were sometimes gathered into extreme fullness. A genuinely ancient garment, these are not now seen except in revived festival dress. Trousers are now the rule. The small-brimmed hat with the round crown is also rare; the usual ones are broader brimmed and flat crowned. The men's jackets are also discreetly decorated. The most heavily embroidered style of both men and women is the *Bigouden* whose red-gold designs in silk, like coiled cord, date from the 1840s; they are copies of motifs on Celtic monuments and were designed purposely for the dress by an embroiderer named Jacob from Quimper.

The area which, after Brittany, has preserved its dress most fully, is Alsace. Although rarely seen during this century as everyday wear, it survived for a long time for Sunday wear and, of course, is to be seen at festival time. The return of Alsace to France in 1918, after fifty years annexation to Germany, caused a revival not entirely authentic in style. The butterfly cap of Strasbourg and its environs was almost universally adopted as a sort of national costume, complete with tricolour rosette, whereas it belongs only to the localities near the capital and a little to the north. There are many styles, varying mostly in the headdress, along the upper Rhine.

The Strasbourg style itself has optional and local alternatives. Besides the bodice laced over an embroidered plastron there is a short, loose jacket, fitting edge to edge with a contrasting band of colour all round. The breast may be covered with a draped shawl or with a broad white frill trimmed round the neckline with a ribbon. The colours, as usual in Alsace, vary according to religion. Red skirts or caps belong to the Catholics, green and black to the Protestants. The butterfly bow need not be plain black or red; it may also be flower-patterned on white or tartan. The bow itself has grown from a more functional bow fastening a ribbon which holds the basic cap in place, and smaller versions are seen elsewhere in Alsace and the neighbouring German territories. In fact, some sort of retaining ribbon or scarf, with or without bows, is common on caps, including fashionable ones, all over Europe.

The young lady from Oberseebach wears the dress appropriate to her age in a village where styles vary, more than anywhere else, according to age and religion. The fabrics are silken, the colours muted, except for the red bows on breast and headdress. In this case the bow merely trims the front of a small black velvet cap, embroidered with sequins and beads, worn high on the head. Her skirt is long and pleated at the back onto a hip yoke while the apron is also decorated with rows of tiny pleats at the top. The sleeves which appear short, are always rolled up. The jewelry is of coral or garnet.

The style worn in Krautgersheim is rather different from the others. Not only is the headdress quite different, but the bodice and skirt are joined and in the same colour. The cap has a rigid crown covered with gold embroidery and beads with a coloured ribbon bow at the nape of the neck. The halo of pleated lace is attached to the edge. The lace collar complements the cap. A good deal of urban refinement has developed in these last styles. Gold embroidered caps seem to be the mark of such development all over the German lands and their neighbours.

The bonnet-shaped cap with the strings, which is clearly not unique to

128 Fisher girl from Boulogne. The frilled bonnet was known as a 'Soleil'. Middle of the nineteenth century.

129 Alsace. This group and the following one show some of the styles to be met with besides that of Strasbourg and its environs, shown on the right.

Alsace, is worn in several localities in the north, often by older women. The men's attire is all much the same with the hat brim sometimes turned up in bicorne and tricorne style, sometimes flat. According to locality, the coat may have buttons or be without.

Auvergne, in the middle of the Massif Central, is a region renowned for its beauty and for its ancient traditions. It has often attracted artists, but unfortunately most of them have been concerned with the landscape rather than the people. The pictorial records that exist showing early forms of the dress depict a rather original style combining elements from the eighteenth and nineteenth centuries in a manner which might once have seemed rather grotesque but now has great charm. Unfortunately, as always, the men's attire consisting of a collarless coat with pleated basque, breeches, gaiters, wooden sabots and a broad hat over long hair, was abandoned long before the women's. However, the sabots, modified versions of the broad hats, and working smocks, remained into the twentieth century. The women's dress was more resilient and even after the Second World War it was possible to see market women wearing the caps belonging to their local dress.

The women's dress consisted of the *bavarel*, a corset which was high and straight across the front and rose to a point behind where it fastened, and worn over a dress with elbow-length sleeves with decorated cuffs. A fringed scarf was tucked into the corset. Over this was worn a large apron with a bib front, the top edge of which was usually decorated and frilled. The skirts were often worn turned up behind to display coloured petticoats and linings. The cap was tulle, goffered along its front edge, the crown gathered and flat at the top. Over the cap it was usual to wear straw hats or poke bonnets with high crowns decorated with black ribbons. In more modern times the hats tended to lose their stylishness and become more bucket-shaped. However, in Bourbonnais, adjacent to the north, the rather similar hats retained their shape. Another headdress worn in Auvergne—a sort of hood with long lappets over the shoulders, was never worn with a hat. The bright but not gaudy colours and the slightly angular silhouette give the dress a quaint dignity. The style survived with modifications well into this century and is revived now at festivals and by folk dance groups to dance the typical *bourrée* of Auvergne.

Borderlands, especially mountainous ones, are usually rich areas for folk dress and the French Pyrennees are no exception. The different valleys have their variations, but the resemblance between the styles and certain garments are typical. La vallée D'Ossau and the area round Eaux Bonnes and Laruns provide good examples. The women's dress lasted well into this century, at least for Sundays, and there was a revival during the 1920s when dance groups were formed. The garment which most attracts attention is the red *capulet*, a long hood, not attached to a cloak, but worn hanging from the top of the head over a tight white cap which has strings under the chin. Under the hood the hair is worn in a plait down the back and may be decorated at the end with small pompoms. Over a white chemise goes a decorative corselet, either waist length or sometimes shaped over the hips with cut tabs. A patterned shawl is worn on top or is often worn with the long ends pulled down through the corselet at the front to hang below the waist. A jacket, shaped to fit closely at the back with cuts below the waist and often too narrow to close at the front, may be worn over the corselet. A skirt and petticoat, one often blue, the other red, come to the ankles revealing light-coloured gaiters like

130 Alsace. In this group we see two examples of bows of smaller size, like the styles across the Rhine in Germany, and two examples of frilled caps. The large halo from Kraut-gersheim edges a bonnet of gold embroidery.

footless stockings. When working in the fields, the long petticoat sometimes used to be discarded and the skirt turned up when the bare knees would be revealed above the gaiters.

The men wear a waistcoat and jacket, both often having wide lapels, breeches and gaiters. The usual footwear is sandals or sabots. In the nineteenth century a variety of hats was worn but the most typical were the large flat beret and the *bonnet,* that is, a bag-like cap hanging to one side. These are the types which have been revived.

The dress is not, in fact, worn any longer in real life. Ski resorts occupy the remote areas at the heads of the formerly isolated valleys and though in some matters village ways and prejudices survive, television has brought its benefits here also.

The Basques

131 Poultry sellers of Álava. *c.* 1870. The method of tying the head-scarf was typical of Basque women.

The Basques, a nation of unique language and mysterious origin, occupy the western Pyrenees and the coastal area adjoining, between Bayonne and Bilbao. About a third of the Basque population live in France in the provinces of Labourd, Basse Navarre and Soule; the remainder in Spain in Guipúzcoa, Vizcaya, Álava and part of Navarra. The area is heavily populated and developed both industrially and for tourism on the coast, with agriculture carried on inland, so the population is not exclusively Basque, nor are the Basques confined to the area. Historically their extended territory spreads into Béarn and the rest of Navarra.

As far as their dress is concerned, though it is difficult to separate it entirely from that of their neighbours, it does have a character of its own. It is typified by simplicity and utility, but also with the sharply contrasting aspects of sombreness or gaiety according to the occasion. We usually see pictures of the Basques—usually the men—engaged in their dances and festive occasions. The white clothes, red sashes, masks, hobby horses, bells and ribbons remind us of our morris dancers and mummers. The Basque dances have been jealously preserved, both as ritual and as a relief to a hard life. In fact, the dress worn for them is rather simple. Apart from certain special uniforms, the clothes are of normal cut with applied trimmings. There are no fine festive clothes of antique Spanish cut as there are in neighbouring Navarra.

In contrast to their capacity for enjoyment the Basques display the deepest show of mourning of almost any European people. Traditional mourning garb for women is a black cloak and large hood. In Spain a caped cloak and hat is prescribed for men, while in France there is a special black smock with a panel attached at the back to be draped over the arm.

For everyday wear the typical headgear for men was the wide flat beret seen elsewhere in the Pyrenees; now usually a small version is worn. A smock, black or blue, and sandals or espadrilles rather than sabots, was the dress of the men in the recent past. The dress of the women was also simple; a sleeved bodice or waistcoat and chemise, the skirt, often turned up, and a neckerchief. The headscarf tied round the head and knotted on top was formerly the mark of the married woman. Girls wore their hair uncovered in two long plaits. For winter, the *kapusaila* (capuchon), a hooded garment like a burnous, gave protection from the weather.

Spain

132 Women of Hecho, showing details of the collar and sleeves of the chemise as well as the fastening of the *basquina*. This dress is now only preserved in the local museum as the village was sacked in 1819.

Economic development has, as elsewhere, brought the active wearing of folk dress almost to an end so that it appears now mainly at Candlemas, Carnival and the great fairs and festivals. The looms, a feature of country households, have mostly gone or stand idle, some with unfinished work still set up. What little production there is, is designed for the tourist and luxury trade. Embroidery, also, in brighter colours than traditional, finds its way on to the international market rather than the garments of the ordinary people. The garments worn at festivals may, in fact, be specially made, especially those for children and for organized groups, but they

may well be genuinely old, brought out from their chests by the grandchildren of the original owners. Time is taking its toll of such garments and of the traditions which have preserved them.

When Ruth M. Anderson made her journeys to Spain to examine the folk dress for the Hispanic Society of America, between 1924 and 1949, she found that, although there were still rich resources in the villages, the living tradition was losing ground and that, especially at the later date, local experts had to collect up ensembles from different households and find models to wear them correctly. After another generation or two people with the necessary memory for such details will be fewer and soon will not be available at all, so the record she made is invaluable to the English speaking student. Fortunately, also, there are costume and handicraft societies, dance groups and local museums which will be able to show the riches of the past.

133 Salamanca. From William Bradford's *Sketches of the Country, Character and Costume in Portugal and Spain*, 1810.

134 Castille. Men of Segovia. The jacket of appliquéd leather is notable, as is the footwear.

135 Peasant of Murcia. Middle of the nineteenth century. He wears the local variant of the *montero* hat. This was once widespread in Spain. The homespun plaid, rather than a cloak, is typical of Murcia.

The pictorial record is rather rich, especially for the nineteenth century when native artists paid attention to the people as subjects for their paintings. From Goya onwards the record is valuable and from mid-century to the end, artists like Valeriano Dominguez Becquer, Ignacio Zuluoga, Joaquín Sorolla and Eduardo Chicharro above all have the combination of detachment from and involvement with their subjects which brings them to life. Among foreign artists, Gustave Doré is probably the best known. He visited Spain several times and knew it well, but the illustrations which appear in several books are, as always, too morbidly occupied by the sordid.

To come to the regions themselves we can, with advantage, start in the north having crossed, as it were, the Pyrenees from France. The prospect before us is very different from that left behind. Although the varieties of Spanish dress are numerous and the details dauntingly varied to describe they have, nevertheless, a national character which is recognizable but difficult to pin-point in a word. Perhaps *mannered* might suffice. A certain angularity and stiffness; a strangeness of proportion seem to characterize it.

Adjoining the Basque provinces and originally part of them is Navarra. At Roncal a rather plain but effective festival dress is worn. The men wear black waistcoats, breeches and stockings. The breeches open at the bottom, as often in the north to show white under-breeches at the knee. These are, in fact, the successors of the original homespun garment of the Spanish peasant and have been retained although the breeches and gaiters of the eighteenth century were adopted by the peasants of Spain, as indeed they were in much of Europe. A purple sash and a white jacket complete the Roncalese dress. The women wear two woollen skirts, both blue, the upper one turned up to reveal a broad red facing. The bodice, sleeveless in summer and long-sleeved in winter, is black. The mantilla, half circular and red with a light border, hangs as far as the waist. In the north mantillas are of cloth rather than lace. As here, they often have a tassel in the middle of the forehead.

Also in the Pyrenees, in the north of Old Aragon, we find two related examples of female dress unlike others in Spain. Both at Ansó and Hecho in neighbouring valleys, the *basquina* is worn, hanging long and full from a small yoke. In Ansó it is green (red for children) with a black yoke over a chemise with a frilled collar, the sleeves enclosed below the elbow in tight oversleeves. For church, a second, black dress is worn on top and for important occasions yet a third, pleated and divided up the middle to be folded back and fastened behind. The braided hair is entirely covered by ribbons bound on like a rope and wound round the head. The mantilla is rectangular, green or white and crossed over the face, a tassel hanging in the centre. The dress of Hecho is often also worn girded back. The upper sleeves of the Hecho chemise are laterally pleated.

Galicia, in the extreme north-west, is a rather separate region somewhat related to Portugal which used to be a dependency centuries ago. It is a region of small farms and markets selling produce so that, as in Portugal, there is much transporting of goods on the heads of the women. The most characteristic items of attire are the sugar-loaf hats of the men, called *montero(s),* which take on a variety of shapes according to district by having the brims turned up or down and cut and twisted into points. This style with local variations was once wide-spread in Spain. Here also the white under-breeches of the men, which may be worn alone for work,

136 Extramadura. Young man in the festival dress of Montehermoso, photographed in 1949.

137 Galicia. Girl from the province of Betanzos. From *Collección de trajes* by Cruz Cano y Olmedilla, 1777.

show below the breeches. In some districts the breeches, though open as usual at the knee, would be close fitting if buttoned up. In others, as at Lugo, the lower opening is straighter and wider, bound with ribbon. At Ordenes the fastenings are on the lower thigh and the opening extends below the knee. Women's dress is rather variable. The laced bodice shown in the engraving by Cruz Cano is not much worn, if at all nowadays. Shawls crossed on the breast are usual and for festive wear, the *dengue,* a stiff little cape with long points, crossed and fastened behind, replaces the shawl. The straw or reed cape worn by country men against the rain is an ancient garment, apparently most effective for its purpose, especially with a large bright cotton umbrella. The cape is also seen in northern Portugal.

Leon, including Salamanca, especially the latter area, presents festive costumes of great richness, both of fabric and decoration. They are dark coloured near the city of Salamanca, brightly coloured in La Ribera, and most heavily bedecked in La Alberca. At La Ribera, the chief characteristic is variety of colour, texture and decoration. The homespun chemise, embroidered in black wool and trimmed at the wrist with knitted lace, is worn with a *manteo,* a conical skirt wrapped over at the back without a seam and decorated both round the hem and up the edge which

138 Girls in the festival dress of Montehermoso, taken in 1949. The shoes are modern, but the garments were already very old.

shows. Round the shoulders is worn a cape, *dengue*, also embroidered. The hair is arranged in *picaporte* (doorknocker) style, with a braid arranged as a chignon at the back. At Candelario the hairstyle reaches its most exaggerated height with the chignon leaning forward on top of the head.

The *vistas* dress of La Alberca depends for its effect on the rigid formality of its stiff conical shape, the top skirt banded with broad appliqué stripes in different colours and materials. A second skirt shows below it. The astonishing item is the weight and mass of jewelry worn across the front on cords from the shoulder blades and hanging halfway to the knees. A man from La Alberca may wear a blue velvet waistcoat, blue or black velvet long breeches like three-quarter length trousers and white stockings. The hat is the broad-brimmed hat of Cordoba, with a medium flat crown, or a knotted kerchief may be worn. The attire for men elsewhere in Salamanca includes a lower cut waistcoat with a decorative panel and silver buttons down each side.

The dress of Extramadura is related in the northern part at least to that of Salamanca, but further south the regional characteristics become more pronounced. In the south of the region, for instance, where the centre is Badajos, the striped homespun cloths give quite a different character to the dress. Extramadura is sheep grazing country and, consequently, the dress of the men reflects their chief occupation. Although the festive dress resembles that of other parts of Spain, with regional differences in the cut of waistcoats and styles of breeches among other items, recent versions when the older form is not available or not favoured are likely to consist of corduroy trousers and short smocks. However, the traditional dress

139 Dancer and Musicians of Galicia. Racinet, 1888.

144

Switzerland. Couple from Schwyz. Early 19th century
Schweiz. Paar aus dem Kanton Schwyz. Frühes 19. Jahrhundert
Suisse. Couple de Schwyz. Debut de XIXe siècle

Italy. Woman and shepherd from Mascione, Abruzzo. 1900
Italien. Frau und Schäfer aus Mascione in den Abruzzen. 1900
Italie. Femme et berger de Mascione dans les Abruzzes. 1900

Spain. Woman from Hecho, Pyrenees and man from Robleda, Salamanca, 19th century
Spanien. Frau aus Hecho, Pyrenäen, und Mann aus Robleda, Salamanca. 19. Jahrhundert
Espagne. Femme de Hecho dans les Pyrénées et homme de Roblède, Salamanque. XIXᵉ

Portugal. Festival dress from Minho Province
Portugal. Festtagsgewand aus der Provinz Minho
Portugal. Costume de fête de la province de Minho

incorporates breeches and gaiters, either of cloth or of decorated leather. These leather garments, the gaiters, the waistcoats, the tabards and leg overalls are of particular interest. The leg overalls and gaiters attract most decoration, but leather appliqué is also employed on cloth jackets and waistcoats. The traditional hat is the conical crowned *calañés*, but since none have been made for many years, hats of many varieties are encountered.

From several localities with individual styles that of Montehermoso is worth describing. Here the dress of the women has its own particular shape and silhouette. The rather short, wide skirts, of which several are worn in different colours, the hems all faced with contrasting material, are not only closely pleated, but are tucked and corded round the lower part in several rows, so that they stand out behind rather suddenly. Shawls or crossed, narrow capes are worn and sometimes a voluminous headcloth. However, the strangest item is the bonnet worn by women, decorated according to age and status. It is a poke bonnet of the most exaggerated style of the nineteenth century, balanced high on the head above a kerchief. Though elaborately decorated with coloured wool, a mirror and straw plaits, it is not properly a part of the festival dress, but a hat worn for going out. The festive headdress is the kerchief alone, and for the rest, a special embroidered jacket and a prodigious quantity of skirts. The hats are still made by the Montehermoso Co-operative, mostly for tourists, as only a very few elderly women continue to wear them and, therefore, the elaborate trimming is not required. A similar, plainer hat is worn at Avila in Castille and one is also reminded of the bonnets of the Auvergne and Bourbonnais in France.

We find another novel silhouette in New Castille, in Toledo Province at Lagartera, the home of Toledo embroideries. Here the cloth of the skirt is retained in pleats by stitching as far as the lower hip, where it is released and encouraged to flare out by the stiffening effect of the decorative bands applied to the lower part of the skirt. For festive wear the line is the same, but not only is the material finer and the embroidery lavish, but pendant ribbons from head and shoulders and elaborate jewelry are added as well. Stockings, red or white, are embroidered with clocks. The notable feature of the dress of the Lagarteran man is his collarless embroidered white shirt, though this may be replaced or covered by a collarless white waistcoat with a black edge at the neck, the fastenings quite concealed.

In the region of Valencia, on the Mediterranean coast, we come not only to a warmer climate, but also to a region of softer clearer colours which are found also in the festive dress. Elegance is the keynote of the women's dress with long, flowered brocade skirts, silk bodices with lace ruffles at the elbow, embroidered net fichus being worn as by fine ladies of the eighteenth century. The hairstyle has side coils with a comb on each side of the head and a high comb behind. The old festive dress of the men would be of velvet in light colours or, alternatively, would be a version of the working dress of the district, the white shirt and white linen loose breeches worn, however, with brightly coloured silken accessories.

In Murcia, also, the white clothes and checked and striped homespuns of the peasant workers contrast with silken garments, for this province was an ancient centre of the silk industry.

We come, at last, to Andalusia. The ruffled gown, so typical, is a product of the nineteenth century and has gone through a number of fashionable modifications, even becoming short in the 1920s. Its present line dates back really to the 1930s, where it was fixed somewhat by the gypsies and professional dancers. The dancers also developed the use of the large fringed shawl wound tightly round the body. Though large Manila shawls were once popular, the ordinary shawl is much smaller. The large combs and the lace mantillas are familiar to everyone. The men of Andalusia affect a certain proud smartness, helped by the sharp, hard lines of the Cordoban hat, formerly the almost universal style. As in Extramadura, the occupations of stock control, in this case of cattle, affect very much the dress and the decorated accessories of leather which belong to the professional herdsmen are used also by riders in the *feria* and during preliminary bullfighting trials. The leg overalls which we have already met in Extramadura, consist of a kind of apron, in Andalusia worn rather high at the front and divided below the groin into two 'legs' which are strapped round the legs of the wearer, somewhat like the *chaps* of the American cowboy. Thus they provide protection and decoration and, because of the tightness at the waist and the long smooth line thus produced, the manly figure is improved.

The improvement of the figure and its surface adornment is carried to extremes by the bullfighters whose dress, upon inspection, is clearly related to the older versions of Spanish dress, especially to that of Seville and Madrid.

140 Galicia. Man in a straw rain cape. Such capes have been worn from early times and are still to be seen in this area and in neighbouring Portugal.

Portugal

141 A local festival. The print dates from 1873 and shows many typical elements of Portuguese dress, some of which still survive.

Portugal, now a republic, has been an independent kingdom for many centuries and, at the height of its development in the fifteenth century, was a world power with a great empire, most of which it retained until recent times. Yet, although this meant great prosperity for a few, the majority of the people have always been poor. Portugal is a beautiful and reasonably fertile country, but unable to support the population

adequately on the land. Consequently, she has been one of the most backward countries in Europe, on a level with Albania and southern Italy. Even in the republic up to 1970 there was little attempt to bring in modern developments in technology to the benefit of the people. In the early 1970s only one third of the households, both urban and rural, had electricity. It is too early to see what effect the latest political developments will have on the lives of the peasantry but they will no doubt be drastic and bring Portugal at last into modern times.

Meanwhile, we have a people, who in large parts of rural Portugal, still live as they did fifty years ago. The dress of these people has not developed much since the nineteenth century. With certain local differences there is a fairly uniform style throughout the country, yet not always a sufficient uniformity within a locality to differentiate it positively from its neighbours. Some areas, however, do have their own styles or colour schemes which mark them out. If we look at nineteenth century prints we shall see that the women's dress incorporates the stiff bodice inherited from the eighteenth century and earlier. In more recent photographs and up to the present time we see that bodices, if worn, have become less rigid but otherwise the dress is much the same, consisting usually of rather voluminous skirts, sometimes girded round the hips so that a fold of the skirt may be drawn up between waist and hip rather than being turned up at the bottom. A kerchief is worn over the head, hanging loose or knotted round the neck, and on top of it a hat. Whereas earlier the women's hats were as wide as the men's, they have tended to shrink to a sort of pork pie shape. Sometimes modern men's hats are worn. Portuguese women have a remarkable talent for carrying things in containers on their heads, ranging from chickens to children. Even today in large cities, market women will convey their produce in this manner. If the load is light enough, the hat may be retained; otherwise a coil of cloth is worn as a pad to make a foundation for the load. The hat, formerly worn by women everywhere, is now seen more in the south; in the north the kerchief is usually worn alone. The older dress of the men of which some of the elements are retained consists of a shirt and waistcoat with buttoned breeches and gaiters. If the gaiters were not worn, the longer under-trousers would show below the knee. Various kinds of wide hat or stocking caps formed the headgear. Oswald Crawfurd writing as 'John Latouche' in *Travels in Portugal,* 1875 says, 'The women have retained their national dress, and in the remoter parts, the men also; but in many places the latter are less conservative, and wear wide-awake hats, trousers and short jackets in lieu of the old national costume'. This 'new' dress was the dress of the richer classes of Spain and Portugal and now forms the festival dress in some areas, notably in Minho province.

The occupational dress of Portugal retains most of all the style of former times. For instance, the shepherds of the Serra da Estrella wear a black suit with buttoned breeches and gaiters. The *campinos* (farmers) of the Alentejo, in particular in the Tagus area, the Ribatejo wear as their traditional winter dress a sheepskin jacket and leg-overalls and, for additional protection, a large cloak. Cloaks, like the fashionable travelling cloaks of the eighteenth century, large shawls and hooded mantles are widely worn by the peasantry. Even today, when there are many ready-made clothes, the large woollen shawls of the women are often spun and woven at home. By contrast, the festive dress of the peasant of the Ribatejo consists of dark breeches, a red-fronted waistcoat, a black jacket rarely

148

worn, and a green stocking cap, the usual male headgear in Portugal, in various colours, when the wide 'Spanish' hat is not worn.

The women of this area wear a long chemise with skirts over the top or, alternatively, a short blouse, a decorative apron and a kerchief with, sometimes, a straw hat. This is the festival dress. Not far away in the district of Leiria the dress is more colourful, the dark skirt having a wide band of red at the hem. The blouse may be of any colour but the kerchief worn under the typical hat is usually deep yellow.

Another occupational dress is that of the fishermen, who in certain localities have adopted a colourful costume. At Nazaré, in Estramadura,

142 Portuguese market woman. The women of Portugal are noted for their skill in balancing bulky articles.

149

the men and sometimes the women sport materials in large checks, originally imported from Britain, but soon made in Portugal to satisfy local demand. Shirts, trousers and blouses may be made of it, though a good deal of black is also worn. Here too, the men have the baggy cap, this time in black; it serves the fisherman as pocket and hold-all. The women normally wear kerchiefs, but for best have the typical Portuguese hat with a veil behind and a large pompom at the front. At Povoa de Varzim, north of Oporto, the fishermen wear light coloured trousers and jerseys with patterns and motifs of a marine inspiration. The stocking cap here is red and very voluminous.

In the hilly eastern province of Beira we find a functional dress suited to the exposed countryside. William Bradford, travelling in 1808–9, described and indeed illustrated it as employing no other colours than blue and brown and his picture depicts a female figure so wrapped up in her cloak that no details are visible. His description is more or less true today. The dress of the women near Guarda, the highest town in Portugal, consists of a short skirt over a chemise with thick woollen stockings, often blue, and a bodice and apron. As protection against the weather a hooded mantle covers the head and hangs below the waist.

To return to the north west and Minho province the other important costume there, indeed the most colourful in Portugal, is that of Viana do Castelo and its surrounding area. Here the men, as described by Latouche, wear the rather formal black suit with sets of silver buttons curving across the front and round the cuffs for festive occasions. The suit is lined in red and may have a sash in red or blue according to locality or the dress of the partner. Clearly, though far from well-off, the people here have always preferred to display their little wealth on their backs. For the same reason, the women wear their dowries in the form of as much gold jewelry of heavy antique design as they can afford. The dress of the women, though always similar in composition, varies in colour according to village and in individual design according to the wearer, who makes her own. However, the two main colour schemes are the so-called *red* and *blue*. The foundation of both is a linen chemise with blue embroidery mainly on the shoulders. In the *red* dress, the homespun skirt, patterned, often vertically striped at the top and closely pleated just below the waist, has a plain red, black or dark blue lower part, sometimes with decoration round the hem. The bodice is also in two colours, black at the waist and red above, both parts usually covered with coloured embroidery. The apron is especially thick and heavy and woven in formal, sometimes geometric patterns in several colours. A fringed shawl is worn on the shoulders and a fringed kerchief twisted and tied on the head. The *blue* dress is much more sober, in fact, mostly black, but with a flowered apron and patterned kerchief. The bridal dress is, in fact, black but of rich cloth relieved with gold embroidery, the white lace of the headdress and the gold jewelry, as always. The gold jewelry is so much an integral part of the apparel that it is worn throughout periods of mourning though lightly covered by a veil. White stockings, sometimes footless, and delicate embroidered mules are the appropriate wear for best or dancing. For work wooden-soled mules or tall boots are worn though bare feet, frowned on by the government, are preferred.

The Minho province not only adjoins Spanish Galicia but the local dialects of each are related and so is the dress. There is much trafficking across the border. Here, as in Galicia, may still be seen the curious straw or

143 A *campino* of Alentejo, about 1950, wearing leg overalls and waistcoat of sheepskin.

reed cape as protection against the weather.

There is in Portugal a good deal of ritual costume to accompany special dances and festivities. In several localities, including Lisbon, there are sword and morris dances connected with carnival and midsummer. A particularly interesting ritual dance survives in Tras os Montes in the extreme north east. In the town of Miranda the men perform a stick dance, a form of morris in a ribboned and flowered costume, the most extraordinary item of which is a long starched petticoat, not a long shirt worn loose, but in fact a petticoat adopted from women's dress.

144 Torres Vedras, 1808–9. From William Bradford's *Sketches of the Country, Character and Costume in Portugal and Spain*, 1810.

145 Fisherwomen from Oporto, 1875.

Illustration acknowledgments

Archive Fokhar, Sofia 26, 27, 29, 30
Baran, Ludvik 1, 2
Contact, Amsterdam 86 (Cas Oorthuys)
Corvina, Budapest 12
Danube Travel 11, 18
Doaré, Jos le 123
Editions Tatran, Bratislava 7, 8 (Alexander Paul)
Fremdenverkehrsband, Schwarzwald 96 (Karl Müller)
Gallery of West Bohemia, Pilsen 9
Hassing Publishers, Copenhagen 80 (Inga Aistrup)
Hispanic Society of America 136, 138
Instituto P. Sarmiento de Estudios Gallegos, Santiago 140
Ioanna Papantoniou 43, 44
Landesfremdenverkehrsamt, Klagenfurt 110 (Oefyw-Markowitsch), 111 (Reinhold Kandolf Hermager)
Landesmuseum, Karlsruhe 102, 103
Landesverkehrsamt in Salzburg 104, 106 and 107 (LVA Salzburg)
Langewiesche, Karl Robert 98 (Erich Retzlaff)
Lorenz, Lutz 94
Mainfränkisches Museum, Würzburg 99
Matica Slovenská, Martin 5
Messageries Paul Kraus, Luxemburg (Ville) 92
Mestské Museum v Domažlicich, Domažlice 3
Moravské Museum, Brno 6
Museum of Popular Art, Bucharest 22
Nakladatestú Petrov, Brno 4 (J. Fiala)
National Ethnographical Museum, Warsaw 56 and 60 (Krysztof Chojnacki), 58 and 59 (Bohdan Czarnecki)
Nationalmuseet, Brede 79, 80a
National Museum, Prague 10
National Museum of Finland, Helsinki 72 (U.T. Sirelius), 73 and 74 (István Rácz)
National Museum of Switzerland 115, 116
National Tourist Organization of Greece 41, 47
Norsk Folkemuseum, Oslo 62, 63, 65
Publications Ortiz Echague, Madrid 132, 134
Real Academia Española 131
Romania State Publishing House 20
Romanian Tourist Office 24
Secretariado Nacional Da Informaçao 143
Stadt Archiv Kempten 100
Swiss National Tourist Office 112 (Plattner), 117 (Maximilien Brugmann)
Thames and Hudson 37 (Tošo Dabac)
VEB Domawina Verlag, Bautzen 95, 97
Veleva, Maria 25, 28
Vita Nova 85

Bibliography

BIBLIOGRAPHICAL WORKS OF COSTUME

COLAS, René. *Bibliographie général du costume et de la mode*. 2 vols. Paris, 1933, Reprinted New York, Hacker, 1963.

DEMOS. *Internationale ethnographische und folkloristische Informationen*. Berlin: Akademie Verlag, quarterly since 1960.

HILER, Hilaire and HILER, Meyer. *Bibliography of costume*. New York, Wilson, 1939.

LIPPERHEIDE, Franz Joseph, Freiherr von. *Katalog der Freiherrlich Lipperheideschen Kostümbibliothek*. 2 vols. Berlin, 1896 1905.

Staatliche Museen, Berlin, Kunstbibliothek. *Katalog der Lipperheideschen Kostümbibliòthek*. 2 vols. Rev. ed. by Evan Nienholdt and Gretel Wagner. Berlin, Mann, 1965. New York, Hacker, 1967.

MONRO, Isabel S. and COOK, D. E. (eds.). *Costume index*. New York, Wilson, 1937. Supplement 1957.

VICTORIA and ALBERT MUSEUM, London. *A list of works on costume in the National Art Library*. London: Eyre and Spottiswoode, 1881.

WILDHABER, Robert. *International folklore and folklife bibliography*. Bonn, Rudolf Habelt Verlag, 1972.

GENERAL WORKS

BLÄTTER FÜR KOSTÜMKUNDE, *Historische und Volks-Trachten*. 2 vols. Berlin, Lipperheide, 1876–78.

BRUHN, W. and TILKE, M. *A pictorial history of costume*. London, Zwemmer, 1955.

GILBERT, John. *National costumes of the world*. London, Hamlyn, 1972.

HAMMERTON, J. A. (ed.). *Peoples of all nations*. 7 vols. London, Educational Book Co. 1922–24.

HUXLEY, Francis. *Peoples of the world in colour*. London, Blandford, 1964.

LANTÉ, Louis Marie. *Costumes des femmes de Hambourg, du Tyrol, de la Hollande, de la Suisse, de la Franconie, de l'Espagne, du royaume de Naples . . .* Paris: 1827.

LECOMPTE, Hippolyte. *Costumes européens*, Paris, Delpech, 1817–19.

MANN, Kathleen. *Peasant costume in Europe*. London, Black, 1950.

RACINET, A. *Le costume historique*. 6 vols. Paris, Firman-Didot, 1888.

STOP [i.e. L.P.G.B. Morel-Retz] *Costumes nationaux*. Paris, Hautecoeur-Martinet, n.d.

TILKE, M. *Costumes of Eastern Europe. Osteuropaische Volkstrachten in Schnitt und Farbe*. London: Benn. Berlin: Wasmuth, 1925.

TILKE, M. *Costume patterns and designs*. London, Zwemmer, 1956.

WAHLEN, Auguste. *Moeurs, usages et costumes de tous les peuples du monde—Europe*. Brussels, 1844.

The Austro-Hungarian Empire

GAUL, Franz. *Österreichisch-ungarische National-Trachten*. Vienna, Lechner, 1881–88.

HOLME, Charles, (ed.). *Peasant art in Austria and Hungary*. London, Studio, 1911.

JASCHKE, Franz. *National-Kleidertrachten und Ansichten von Ungarn, Croatien, Slavonien, dem Banat, Siebenburgen und der Bukowina*. Vienna, Strauss, 1821.

LEPAGE-MEDVEY, E. *National Costumes*. Paris, Hyperion, 1939.

MOLEVILLE, M. Bertrand de. *The costume of the hereditary states of the House of Austria*. London, Miller, 1804

MUSÉE COSMOPOLITE. *Allemagne et Autriche*. Paris, 1850–63.

RANFTL, Kollarz, GERASCH and KALIWODA (illustrators). *Trachten—Album nach der Natur gezeichnet und lithographiert von: Ranftl, Kollarz, Gerasch and Kaliwoda*. Vienna, Paterno, n.d.

VALÉRIO, Theodore. *Costumes de la Hongrie et des provinces danubiennes*. Paris, 1885.

Czechoslovakia

GENERAL WORKS

KOVARNA, František (ed.). *Mánesův odkaz národu zemi milovane*. Prague, Orbis, 1940.

MÁNES, Josef. *Venkov Josef Mánesa*. Prague, Muller, 1940.

REY, J. and TMEJ, Zdeněk. *The world of dance and ballet in Czechoslovakia*. Prague, Artia: London, Spring Books.

ŠMIROUS, Karel, and ŠOTKOVÁ, Blažena. *National costumes of Czechoslovakia*. Prague, Artia, [1956].

TYRŠOVÁ, Renata, and HANTICH, Henri. *Le paysan tchèque*. Paris and Prague, 1911.

VÁCLAVÍK, Antonín, and OREL, Jaroslav. *Textile folk art*. Prague, Artia. London, Spring Books, [1956].

BOHEMIA

ŠOTKOVÁ, Blažena. *Naše lidové kroje*. 8 parts. Prague, Vyšehrad, 2nd edn. 1951.

STRÁNSKÁ, Drahomíra. *Lidové kroje v Československu. 1. Čechy*. Prague, Otto, 1949.

MORAVIAN SLOVAKIA

BOGATYREV, Petr. *The functions of folk costume in Moravian Slovakia*. The Hague, Mouton, 1971.

UPRKA, Joža. *Joža Uprka k pátému výočí umělcovy smrti* Ed.   Štepán Jež. Prague, Sfinx, 1944.

ŠEVELA, Martin. *U žúdra*. Brno. Nakladatelství Petrov, n.d.

SLOVAKIA

Bibliography

KUBOVÁ, Milada. *Bibliografia slovenskej etnografie a folklorisiky za roky 1960–1969*. Bratislava, Národopisný ústav SAV, 1971. Annual additions.

STANO, Pavol. *Bibliografia slovenského ľudového výtvarného umenia. I. to 1957. II. 1958–68*. Martin: Matica slovenská, 1959, 1970.

General Works

BARTOŇOVÁ, Božena. *Ludový odev z Madunic v zbierkach vlastivedného múzea v Hlohovci*. 1969.

DUBNICKA, Elena. *Peter M. Bohůn; život a dielo*. Bratislava, 1960.

KOVAČEVIČOVÁ, Soňa. *Ľudový odev v Hornom Liptove*. Bratislava, 1955.

MARKOV, J. *The Slovak national dress through the centuries*. Prague, Artia, 1956.

MRLIAN, Rudolf (ed.). *Slovak folk art—architecture, costumes and embroideries*. Prague, Artia, 1953.

NOVOTNÝ, V. *Mánes a Slovensko*. Bratislava, 1952.

PÁTKOVÁ, Jarmila. *Ľudový odev v okolí Trnavy*. Bratislava, 1957.

PRANDA, Adam (ed.). *Slovenský ľudový textil*. Martin: Osveta, 1957.

VYDRA, Josef. *Indigo blue print in Slovak folk art*. Prague, Artia, 1954.

SUDETENLAND

MALLY, Fritzi. *Deutsche Trachten aus den Sudetenländern*. Introduction by Josef Hanika. Prague, Volk und Reich, 1943.

Hungary

GENERAL WORKS

BÁTKY, Zsigmond, and GYÖRFFY, István. *L'art populaire Hongrois*. Budapest, 1928.

BÁTKY, Zsigmond, GYÖRFFY, István and VISKI, Károly. *A magyarság néprajza. 1. Viselet*. Budapest, 1941.

BIKKESSY, Joseph Heinbucher Edler von. *Pannoniens Bewohner in ihren volkstümlichen Trachten*. Vienna, 1816–20.

FÉL (ed.), HOFER, T. and CSILLÉRY, K. *Hungarian peasant art*. Budapest, Corvina, 1958.

GÁBORJÁN, A. *Hungarian peasant costumes*. Budapest, Corvina: London, Clematis, 1969.

GINK, Károly and KISS, Ivor Sándor. *Folk art and folk artists in Hungary*. Budapest, Corvina: London, Clematis, 1968.

GYÖRFFY, István. *A cifra szür*. Budapest, 1930.

HUNGARIAN ETHNOGRAPHICAL MUSEUM. *Hungarian folk art*. Budapest, Corvina, 1954.

KORNISS, Péter. *Heaven's bridegroom: Hungarian folk art*. Budapest, Corvina, 1975.

KRESZ, Mária. *Magyar parasztviselet, 1820–1827*. Budapest, 1956.

MALONYAY, Dezsö. *A magyar nép müvészete*. 5 vols. Budapest, Franklin, 1907–22.

NEMES, Mihály. *A magyar viseletek története*. Budapest, Franklin, 1900.

ORTUTAY, Gyula. *A magyar népmüvészet*. 2 vols. Budapest, Franklin, 1941.

PALOTAY, G. and KONECSNI, G. *Hungarian folk costumes*. Budapest, Officina, 1938

PIFFL, Erna. *Deutsche Bauern in Ungarn*. Berlin, Grenze, 1938.

SZENTIVÁNI, G. *Magyar mosoly. Népünk müvészi viselete*. Budapest, 1942.

UJVÁRINÉ KERÉKGYÁRTO, A. *A magyarnöi haj- és fejviselet*. Budapest, 1932.

VARJASI, R. and HORVATH, V. *Hungarian rhapsody: the Hungarian State Folk Ensemble*. Budapest, Corvina, 1956.

VISKI, Károly. *Hungarian peasant customs*. Budapest, Vajna, 1932.

THE GREAT PLAIN

BÉRES, A. *A debreceni cifra szür*. Budapest, 1955.

TRANSDANUBIA

DÖMÖTÖR, S. *Örség*. Budapest, 1960.

KATONA, Imre. *Sárköz*. Budapest, 1962.

KODOLÁNYI, J. *Ormánság*. Budapest, 1960.

VAJKAI, A. *Balatonmellék*. Budapest, 1964.

THE UPLANDS

DALA, J. and ERÉLYI, T. *Matyóföld*. Budapest, 1941.

GYÖRFFY, István. *Matyó népviselet*. Budapest, 1956.

Romania

GENERAL

AVRAMESCU, Elena. *Broderiile la Romîni*. Bucharest, 1959.

BĂNĂŢEANU, Tancred. *Folk costumes, woven textiles and embroideries of Rumania*. Bucharest, 1958.

BRITISH MUSEUM. *Village Arts of Romania*. London, 1971.

ENĂCHESCU CANTEMIR, Alexandrina. *Portul popular românesc. Romanian folk costumes*. Craiova, Scrisul Românesc, 1939.

ENĂCHESCU CANTEMIR, Alexandrina. *Portul popular românesc. Romanian folk costumes*. Bucharest, Meridiane, 1971.

JORGA, N. *L'art populaire en Roumanie, son caractère, ses rapports et son origine*. Paris, 1923.

OPRESCU, Gheorghe. *Peasant art in Roumania*. London, Studio, 1929.

ZDERCIUC, Boris, PETRESCU, Paul, and BĂNĂŢEANU, Tancred. *Folk art in Rumania*. Bucharest, Meridiane, 1964.

MOLDAVIA

FLORESCU, Florea Bobu. *Portul popular din Ţara Vrancei*. Bucharest, 1958.

FLORESCU, Florea Bobu. *Portul popular din Moldova de Nord*. 1965.

Port, ţesături, cusături. Bucharest: Focşani, 1969.

WALLACHIA

FLORESCU, Florea Bobu. *Portul popular din Muscel*. Bucharest, 1957.

FOCŞA, Gheorghe. *Evolutia portului popular din zona Jiului de Sus*. Bucharest, 1957.

TRANSYLVANIA AND BANAT

PETRESCU, Paul. *Costumul popular romînesc din Transilvania şi Banat*. Bucharest, 1959.

TRANSYLVANIA

Olt Valley Area

IRIMIE, Cornel. *Portul popular din Ţara Oltului—zona Făgăraş*. 1956.

IRIMIE, Cornel. *Portul popular din Ţara Oltului—zona Avrig*. 1957

IRIMIE, Cornel. *Portul popular din Ţara Oltului—zona Perşanilor*. n.d.

Hunedoara and Haţeg

BĂNĂŢEANU, Tancred. *Portul popular din Ţara Oaşului*. Bucharest, 1955.

VUIA, Romulus. *Portul popular al pădurenilor din regiunea Hunedoara*. 1958.

VUIA. Romulus. *Portul popular din Ţara Haţegului*. Bucharest, Meridiane, 1962.

Crişana

DUNĂRE, Nicolae. *Portul popular din Bihor*. 1957.

Arta populară din Sălaj. Zalău, 1969.

MOZEŞ, Tereza. *Portul popular femeiesc din bazinul Crişul Repede*. Oradea, 1968.

THE TRANSYLVANIAN SAXONS

RETZLAFF, Hans (photographer). *Bildnis eines deutschen Bauernvolkes. Die Siebenbürger Sachsen*. Text von Dr. Misch Orend. Berlin and Stuttgart, 1934.

HUNGARIANS IN TRANSYLVANIA

NAGY, J. *A torockói magyar népi öltözet. Portul popular maghiar din Trascău*. Bucharest, 1957.

NAGY, J. *A kalotaszegi magyar népi öltözet*. Bucharest, 1958.

BULGARIANS IN THE BANAT

VEKOVA TELBIZOVA, Maria and TELBIZOV, K. *Narodnata nosiya na banatskite Bulgari*. Sofia, Ethnographical Museum, 1958.

Bulgaria

FILOV, Bogdan D. *Geschichte der bulgarischen Kunst unter der türkischen Herrschaft und in neueren Zett*. Berlin and Leipzig, de Gruyter, 1933.

FOX, Sir Frank. *Bulgaria*. London, Black, 1915.

KATSAROVA, Raina. *Dances of Bulgaria*. London, Parrish, 1951.

NASLEDNIKOVA, Venera. *Istoriya na bulgarskiya kostium*. Sofia, Nauka i Izkustvo, 1970.

STAINOV, P. (ed.). *Kompleksni nauchni expeditsii v zapadna Bulgaria*. Sofia, BAS, 1961.

SPASOVA, Nadezhda. *Pleven. Narodno izkustvo. Album*. Sofia, 1069.

VAKARELSKI, Khristo and IVANOV, D. *Bulgarski narodni nosii, cego i v minaloto*. Sofia, 1942.

VELEVA, Maria G. *Bulgarski narodni nosii i shevitsi*. Sofia, Nauka i Izkustvo, 1950.

VELEVA, Maria G. *Bulgarski narodni nosii*. Sofia, Nauka i Izkustvo, 1956.

VELEVA, Maria G. *Bulgarskata dvuprestilchena nosia*. Sofia, BAS, 1963.

VELEVA, Maria G. *Raznoobrazieto na bulgarskite narodni nosii*. Sofia, Nauka i Izkustvo, 1969.

VELEVA, Maria G. *Technologia i khudozhestveni kachestva na Bulgarskite narodni tekstilni proizvedeniya*. Sofia, 1975.

VELEVA, Maria G., and LEPANTSOVA, Eugenia I. *Bulgarian folk costumes*. 2 vols. Sofia. Bulgarian Academy of Sciences, 1961, 1974. Separate editions in other languages.

Yugoslavia

ARSENOVIĆ, Nikola. *Jugoslovenska narodna nošnja. Costumes nationaux yougoslaves*. Belgrade, Ethnographical Museum, 1930.

BANKFIELD MUSEUM. *The Durham collection of garments and embroideries from Albania and Yugoslavia by Laura E. Start with notes by M. Edith Durham*. 1939.

Costume of Illyria and Dalmatia. Les costumes de l'Illyrie et de la Dalmatie' 2 vols. London, 1824.

ČULIĆ, Zorislava. *Nošnje u Bosni i Hercegovini; Folk costumes in Bosnia and Herzegovina*. Sarajevo, Svjetlost, 1965.

DRAŠKIĆ, Miroslav, V. *Narodne nošnje severo-zapadne Bosne*. Banja-Luka, Ethnographical Department, 1962.

GOPČEVIC, Spiridion. *Makedonien und Alt Serbien*. Vienna, Seidel, 1889.

HACQUET, Balthasar. *L'Illyrie et la Dalmatie: moeurs, usages et costumes des habitants, et de ceux des contrées voisines*. 2 vols. Paris, Nepven, 1815.

HIELSCHER, Kurt. *Picturesque Yugoslavia, Slavonia, Croatia, Dalmatia, Montenegro, Herzegovina, Bosnia and Serbia*. New York, Westermann: London, Studio, 1926.

KIRIN, Vladimir. *Narodne nošnje Jugoslavije*. 4 folders. Zagreb, [1953].

KIRIN, Vladimir. *Narodne plesovi Jugoslavije*. Zagreb, [1958].

KOLUDROVIĆ, Aida. *Ženské varoške nošnje v sjevernoj i srednjoj Dalmaciji*. Split, Ethnographical Museum, 1954.

RIBARIĆ, Jelka Radauš. *The folk costumes of Croatia*. Zagreb, 1975.

Albania

CARTWRIGHT, J. *Selections of the costume of Albania and Greece*. London, [1882].

DURHAM, Mary Edith. *The burden of the Balkans*. London, Arnold, 1905.

HOBHOUSE, J. C. *A journey through Albania and other provinces of Turkey, during the years 1809 and 1810*. London, 1813.

MBORJA, Dhimiter, and ZOJZI, Rrok. *Popular art in Albania*. Tirana, State University, 1959.

NOPCSA, Ferencz. *Albanien: Bauten, Trachten und Geräte Nordalbaniens*. Leipzig, de Gruyter, 1925.

Greece

ARGENTI, Philip, P. *The costumes of Chios*. London, Batsford, 1953.

BENAKI MUSEUM, ATHENS. *Hellenic national costumes*. 2 vols. Athens, 1948, 1954.

CROSFIELD, Domini. *Dances of Greece*. London, Parrish, 1948.

FOKA-KOSMETATOU, K. P. *Foressies*. 1953.

FRAGAKI, Evangelia. *I elliniki laïki techni tis Kritis*. 2 vols. Athens, 1960.

MUSEUM OF GREEK POPULAR ART. *Kentimata kai kosmimata tis ellikinis foressias. Embroidery and ornament on Greek costume*. Athens, 1966.

PAPANTONIOU, Ioanna. *Ellikinis foressies; Greek costumes. 1 Women's dress. 2 Men's dress*. Athens, Aspioti-Elka, 1973.

STACKELBERG, Otto Magnus, Freiherr von. *Trachten und Gebräuche der Neugriechen*. Berlin, Reimer, 1831.

TARSOULI, Athina. *Costumes grecs*. Athens, 1941.

TARSOULI, Athina. *Kentimata kai foressiestis dodecaneson. Embroideries and costumes of Dodecanese*. Athens, 1951.

Russia

BIBLIOGRAPHY

LENIN STATE LIBRARY, Moscow. *Kostium narodov SSSR i zarubezhnych stran*. 1964.

GENERAL WORKS

Costume de l'Empire Russe, représenté en plus de soixante-dix gravures superbement colorées. London, Harding, 1803.

GEORGI, Johann Gottlieb. *Beschreibung aller Nationen der russischen Reichs*. S. Petersburg, Müller, 1776–80.

GOSTELOW, Mary. *Embroidery of all Russia*. London, Mills and Boon, 1977.

HOLME, C. (ed.). *Peasant art in Russia*. London, Studio, 1912.

METROPOLITAN MUSEUM OF ART, NEW YORK. *History of Russian costume*, by L. Efimova and others. New York, 1977.

MUSÉE COSMOPOLITE. *Costumes russes*. Paris, 1850–63.

Picturesque representations of the dress and manners of the Russians. London, Murray, 1814.

PROCHOROV, V. *Materialy po istorii russkikh odezhd i obstanovka zhizni narodnoi*. S. Petersburg, 1881–84.

RABOTNOVA, Irina. *Russkaya narodnaya odezhda*. Moscow, 1964.

SOKOLOVSKAYA, V. *Kostiumy k tantsam narodov SSSR*. Moscow, Iskusstvo, 1964.

TKACHENKO, Tamara Stepanovna. *Narodny tanets*. Moscow, Iskusstvo, 1954.

VINOGRADOVA, N. *Russkii narodny kostium; Russian traditional dress*. N. Vinogradova. Moscow, Izobrazitel'noe Iskusstvo, 1969.

BYELORUSSIA

ALINA, K. *Shest' belorusskikh narodnikh tantsev*. Minsk, Gosizdat, BSSR, 1960.

Narodnoe i prikladnoe iskusstvo Sovetskoi Belorussii. Minsk, Gosizdat BSSR, 1958.

UKRAINE including RUTHENIA

DMITRIW, Olya (comp.). *Ukrainian arts*, compiled by Olya Dimtriw, New York, Ukrainian Youths' League of North America, Inc. 1955.

KUL'CHITSKAYA, E. *Narodnaya odezhda zapadnykh oblastei Uk.SSR*. Kiev, Ac. Sci. 1955.

Ukrainskoe narodnoe iskusstvo—odezhda. Kiev, Izomuzgiz Uk.SSR, 1961.

MAKOVSKIY, Sergei Konstanovich. *Peasant art of Subcarpathian Russia*. Prague, Plamja, 1926.

MOLDAVIAN S.S.R

OSHRUKO, L. *Narodnye tantsy Moldavii*. Kishinev, 1957.

ZEVINA, A. M. and LIVSHITS, M. Ya. *Portul natsional Moldoveneck*. Kishinev, 1960.

CAUCASUS AND TRANSCAUCASIA

KOSVEN, Mark Osipovich (ed.). *Narody Kavkaza*. 2 vols. 1961–2.

GEORGIA

DZHAVRISHVILI, D. *Gruzinskie narodnye tantsy*. Tbilisi, 1958.

ARMENIA

PATRIK, A. N. *Armyanskaya odezhda s drevneishikh vremen do nashikh dnei*. Erevan, 1967.

DAGESTAN

AZAMATOVA, Min-Kutas. *Adygeisky narodny ornament*. Maikop, 1960.

CENTRAL U.S.S.R. Basins of the Don, Volga, and Kama rivers.

Upper Volga

MASLOVA, G. S. *Narodny ornament verkhnovolzhskikh Karel*. Moscow, 1951.

Penza

TSELIKOV, N. and ZAOSTROZHKY, V. *Penzensky ruskii narodny* Penza, 1958.

Bashkir Autonomous Republic

GASKAROV, F. A. *Bashkirskie tantsy*. Ufa, 1958.

Kazan—Tartar Autonomous Republic

VOROB'EV, N. *Kazanskie Tatary*. Kazan, Tatgosizdat, 1953.

Mordovian Autonomous Republic

HEIKEL, Axel Olei. *Mordvalaisten pukula ja kuoseja. Trachten und Muster der Mordvinen*. Helsinki, Finno-Ugrian Society, 1897.

Udmurt Autonomous Republic

BELITSER, Vera. *Narodnaya odezhda Udmurtov*. Moscow, 1951.

BALTIC STATES

SLAVA, M. K. *Kulturno-istoricheskie svyazy pribaltiiskikh narodov po dannym odezhdy.* Moscow, Nauka, 1964.

Lithuania

GLEMŽAITĖ, Mikalina. *Lietuviu tautiniai drabužiai*. Vilnius, 1955.

LINGIS, Yu., SLAVIUNAS, Z. and YAKELAITIS, V. *Litovskie narodnye tantsy*. Vilnius, 1955.

Latvia

LATVIJAS LAUKSAIMNIECIBAS KAMERA. *Novadu tērpi*. Jelgava, 1939; republished by Latvian folk dance group 'Dizdancis', Toronto, 1965.

SLAVA, M. *Latviešu tautas tērpi. Latyshskaya narodnaya odezhda*. Rīgā, 1966.

[*National Costumes of Latvia*] Rīgā. Latvijas valsts izdevnecība. n.d.

Estonia

Estonskaya narodnaya odezhda. Tallinn, Ethnogr. Museum, 1960.

Poland

Atlas Polskich Strojów Ludowych. Polskie Towarzystwo ludoznawcze, 1949 and continuing.

CZARNECKA, Irena. *Folk art in Poland*. Warsaw, Polonia, 1958.

CZASZNICKA, Zofia, and NOWAK, Jadwiga. *Haft i zdobienie stroju ludowego*. Warsaw, Sztuka, 1955.

DOBROWOLSKA, Agnieszka. *Żywotek cieszyński*. Katowice, 1930.

DOBROWOLSKA, Agnieszka, and DOBROWOLSKI, Tadeusz. *Strój, haft i koronka w wojewodztwie śląskiem. Le costume populaire, la broderie et la dentelle en Silésie polonaise*. Cracow, Wydawnictwa Śląskie, 1936,

KOTULA, Franciszek. *Poszukiwanie metryk dla stroju ludowego*. Rzeszów, 1954.

MANUGIEWICZ, Jan. *Polskie stroje ludowe*. Warsaw, Centralny Dom Twórczości Ludowej. [1956].

MODZELEWSKA, Feodora. *Stroje ludowe Warmii i Mazur*. Olsztyn, 1958.

PRZEWORSKA, Janina. *Ubiory ludowe*. Warsaw, 1954.

SEWERYN, Tadeusz. *Parzenice góralskie. Les broderies appelées 'parzenice' sur les costumes des montagnards polonais*. Cracow, Ethn. Museum, 1930.

SEWERYN, Udziela. *Ludowe stroje Krakowskie i ich krój. Les costumes des paysans de la région de Cracovie et leur coupe*. Cracow, Ethn. Museum, 1930.

SEWERYN, Udziela. *Hafty Kurpiowskie*. Cracow, Ethn. Museum, 1936.

STRYJEŃSKA, Zofia. *Polish peasant costumes*. Nice, Szwedzicki, 1939.

ZIENKOWICZ, Léon. *Les costumes du peuple polonais*. Paris, Strasbourg, Leipzig, 1841.

Scandinavia

GENERAL WORKS

MUSÉE COSMOPOLITE. *Suède, Norvège et Danemark*. Paris, 1850–63.

PRIMMER, Kathleen. *Scandinavian peasant costume*. London, Black, 1939.

Norway

BIBLIOGRAPHY

LANDSNEMNDA FOR BUNADSSPØSMÅL, OSLO. *Norkse bunader; kjelder, rekonstruksjon, bruk*. Oslo, L.F.B.

GENERAL WORKS

FETT, Harry. *Nationaldragter*. Christiania, 1903.

HAUGLID, R. (ed.). *Native art of Norway*. Oslo, Dreyer, 1965.

JUNGMAN, Beatrix, and JUNGMAN, Nico. *Norway*. London, 1905.

LEXOW, Einar. *Joh. F. L. Dreiers Norske folkedragter*. Christiania, 1913.

MUSÉE COSMOPOLITE. *Suède, Norvège and Danemark*. Paris, 1850–63.

NOSS, Aagot. *Johannes Flintoes draktakvarellar*. Oslo, Det Norske Samlaget, 1970.

NOSS, Aagot. *Johannes Flintoes draktakvarellar*. Oslo, Det Norske Samlaget, 1973.

PRAHL, G. *Norges mest eiendommelige bondedragter*. Bergen, 1827–30.

PRAHL, G. *Norske bondedragter*. Bergen, 1848.

SENN, Johann H. *Norsk nationale klædedragter*. Copenhagen, 1812–1815.

STEWART, Janice S. *The folk arts of Norway*. Univ. of Wisconsin, 1953.

TØNSBERG, Niels Christian. *Norske national dragter*. Christiania,1852.

TØNSBERG, Niels Christian, and TIDEMAND, Adolf. *Norske Folkelivsbilleder*. Christiania, 1854.

EAST AND WEST AGDER

KOREN, D. *Nationaldrakter i Vest-Agder*. Kristiansand, 1947.

SKAR, Sigrun. *Mann-og kvinnebunader på Agder*. Kristiansand, 1953.

AKERSHUS

KVAAL, Inger-Marie. *Klededrakt på Romeriksbygdene ca. 1600–1850*. Lillestrøm, 1941.

HORDALAND

HIRTH, Eirik. *Klædebunaden på Voss i eldre og nyare tid*. Bergen, 1945.

STULAND, Gudrun. *Hardangersaum*. Oslo, 1960.

OPPLAND

GJESSING, Thale. *Gudbrandsdalens Folkedrakter*. Oslo, 1949.

ROMSDAL

NERHEIM, Konrad. *Romsdalsbunaden*. Molde, 1926.

Sweden

BIBLIOGRAPHY

SVENSKA UNGDOMSRINGEN FÖR BYGDEKULTUR. *Förteckning över folksdräktslitteratur*. 1968.

GENERAL WORKS

ARNÖ-BERG, Inga and HAZELIUS-BERG, Gunnel. *Folkdräkter och bygdedräkter från hela Sverige*. Västerås, I.C.A., 1976.

CEDERBLOM, Gerda. *Svenska allmogedräkter . . .* Stockholm, Nordiska Museet, 1921.

DAHLSTRÖM, Carl Andreas. *Några minnesblad från Sveriges landsbygd*. Stockholm, 1862.

DAHLSTRÖM, Carl Andreas. *Svenska folkets seder bruk och klädedrägter*. Stockholm, 1863.

HÅRD, A. O. *Svenska folkdrägter. Med tio lithocromierade plancher af Hårdh*. Stockholm, 1854.

NORDISKA MUSEET STOCKHOLM. *Folkdräkter fran sodra Sverige*. Stockholm, Nordiska Museet, 1931.

NORDISKA MUSEET, STOCKHOLM. *Swedish folk dances*. Stockholm, 1939.

NYLÉN, Anna-Maja. *Swedish peasant costumes*. Stockholm, Nordiska Museet, 1949.

Peasant art in Sweden, Lapland and Iceland. London, Studio, 1910.

SANDBERG, J. C. *Ett år i Sverige*. Stockholm, 1827.

SVENSSON, Sigrid. *Folkdräkter från mellersta Sverige*. Stockholm, Nordiska Museet, 1934.

SVENSSON, Sigrid. *Folkdräkter från Dalarna och norra Sverige*. Stockholm, Noridska Museet, 1936.

SVENSSON, Sigrid. *Gammalt dräktsilver*. Västerås, 1964.

WINTZELL, Inga. *Så var barnen klädda*. Stockholm, 1972.

WISTRAND, Per Gustaf. *Svenska folkdräkter*. Stockholm. Nordiska museet, 1907.

DALARNA-DALECARLIA

ALM, Albert. *Dräktalmanach för Leksands socken*. Kalmar, 1923.

ALM, Albert. *Dräktalmanacka för Floda socken i Dalarna*. Stockholm, 1930.

BERGMAN, I. *Krink dräktskicket i Åhl*. Malung, 1969.

EKSTRÖM, Gunnar. *Sockendräkten i Rättvik*. Falun, 1935.

MATTSON-DJOS, E. *Moradräkten*. Mora, 1971.

ODSTEDT, Ella. *Folkdräkter i Övre Dalarne*. Uppsala, 1953.

SÖDERBAUM, Wilhelm. *Leksandsdräktens utveckling under tvåhundra år, 1750–1950*. Tällberg, G. Söderbaum, 1967.

TÄGTSTRÖM, David. *Leksandsdräkten*. Stockholm, Sigma, 1967.

GÄSTRIKLAND

HEDLUND, Greta. *Dräkt och kvinnligslöjd i Ovansjö socken, 1750–1850 talet*. Gävle, 1951.

JÄMTLAND

BJÖRKQUIST, Lennart. *Jämtlands folkliga kvinnodräkter . . .* Uppsala, Appleberg, 1941.

SKÅNE–SCANIA

SVENSSON, Sigrid. *Skånes Folkdräkter. En dräkthistorisk undersökning, 1500–1900*. Stockholm, Nordiska museet, 1935.

WALLGREN, Otto. *Skånska allmogens klädedrägter*. Stockholm, 1860–63.

SMÅLAND

HOFRÉN, Manne. *Sockendräkt och häradsdräkt*. Kalmar, 1927.

SÖDERMANLAND

NYLÉN, Anna-Maja. *Folkigt dräktskick i Västra Vingåker och Österåker*. Stockholm, Nordiska Museet, 1947.

Finland

HEIKEL, Axel Olai. *Die Volkstrachten in den Ostseeprovinzen und in Setukesien*. Helsinki, 1909.

HEIKEL, Yngvar. *Svensk-Finlands bygdedräkter*. 8 parts. Helsinki, 1952–66.

NATIONAL MUSEUM, FINLAND. *Folk costumes and textiles*.

SCHVINDT, Theodor. *Finnische Volkstrachten*. Helsinki, 1905.

SIRELIUS, V. T. *Suomen kansallispukaja*. I and II. Helsinki, Otava, 1921.

VAHTER, Tyyni, and STRANDBERG, Greta. *Suomen kansallispukaja*. Helsinki, Söderström, 1936.

The Lapps

FJELLSTRÖM, Phebe. *Lapskt silver, 1–2*. Stockholm, 1962.

GJESSING, Gjertrud, and GJESSING, Gutorm. *Lappedrakten. Costume of the Lapps*. Oslo, 1940.

SPENCER, Arthur. *The Lapps*. Newton Abbot: David and Charles, 1978.

Denmark

BIBLIOGRAPHY

Bibliografi over dansk folkekultur. Copenhagen, Foreningen Danmarks Folkeminder. 1955 and continuing. Annual classified list.

GENERAL WORKS

ANDERSEN, Ellen. *Folk costumes in Denmark*. Copenhagen, Hassing, 1952.

ANDERSEN, Ellen. *Danske bønders klædedragt*. Copenhagen, Carit Andersen, 1960.

ANDERSEN, Ellen. *Folkedragter i Nationalmuseet*. Copenhagen, National Museum, 1971.

LUND, Frederik Christian. *Danske nationaldragter . . .* Copenhagen, Stinch, 1862.

OTTESEN, Louise. *Danske folkedragter*. Copenhagen, Hasselbach, 1923.

AMAGER

MYGDAL, Elna. *Amagerdragter: vaevninger og syninger*. Copenhagen, Det Schønbergske Forlage, 1932.

STRUNGE, Mogens. *Gamle Amagerdragter*. Copenhagen, Joensen, 1952.

ZEALAND

MØLLER, Jens Schon. *Folkdragter i Nordvestsjælland*. Copenhagen, Det Schønbergske Forlag, 1926.

Iceland

GUDJÓNSSON, Elsa E. *Books and articles wholly or in part concerned with textiles and costumes in the National Museum of Iceland and Icelandic textiles and costumes in general*. Reykjavík: 1972.

BRUUN, Daniel. *Den islandske kvinde og hendes dragt*. Copenhagen, Glydendal, 2nd ed. 1928.

GÍSLADÓTTIR, Gudrún. *Um islanzkan faldbúning med myndum eptir Sigurd málara Gudmundsson*. Kaupmannahöfn, Möller, 1878.

GUDJÓNSSON, Elsa E. *Íslenzkir thjódbúningar kvenna*. Reykjavík, Bókaútgáfa Menningarsjóds, 1969.

JÓNASSON, Jónas. *Íslenzkir thjódhaettir*. Reykjavík, 1934.

THÓRDARSON, Matthias. *Tracht und Schmuck auf Island. Tracht und Schmuck in nordischen Raum, 2.* Leipsig, 1938.

The Netherlands

BING, Valentyn and VON UEBERVELDT, Braet. *Nederlandsche kleederdrachten.* Amsterdam, Frans Buffa en Zonen, 1857.

GARDILANNE, Gratiane de, and MOFFAT, Elizabeth Whitney. *National costumes of Holland.* Harrap, 1932.

GREEVEN, H. *Collection des costumes des provinces septentrionales du royaume des Pays Bas . . .* Amsterdam, Buffa : Paris, Engelmann, 1828.

HIJLKEMA, Riet. *National costume in Holland.* Amsterdam, Meulenhoff, 1951.

KLEDERDRACHTENCOLLECTIE *Koningin Wilhelmina, 1948 1973.* Arnhem, Nederlands Openlucht Museum, 1973.

MAASKAMP, E. *Representations of dresses, morals and customs in the Kingdom of Holland.* Amsterdam, Maaskamp. 1808, 1811, 1829.

MOLKENBOER, Theodoor. *De kleeding van eene vrouw op het eiland Marken.* Amsterdam, [1917].

MUSÉE COSMOPOLITE. *Belgique et Hollande.* Paris, 1850–63.

NEDERLANDS OPENLUCHT MUSEUM. *Het platteland rond Oranje.* Arnhem, N.O.M. 1973.

NEDERLANDS OPENLUCHT MUSEUM. *Van hoofdbrekens en kopzorgen.* Arnhem, N.O.M. 1975.

NIEUWHOFF, Constance. *Onze Klederdrachten.* Wageningen, Zomer en Keuning, 1975.

NIEUWHOFF, Constance. *Klederdrachten.* Amsterdam, Contact, 1976.

SEMPLE. *Costumes of the Netherlands.* London, Ackermann, 1817.

THIENEN, F. W. S. Van and DUYVETTER, J. *Klederdrachten. Traditional Dutch costumes.* Amsterdam, Contact, 1968.

VALETON, Elsa M. *Dutch costumes.* Amsterdam, De Driehoek, 1959.

VRIES, R. W. P. de. *Dutch national costumes.* Amsterdam, Meulenhoff, [1930].

Belgium

MADOU, Jean Baptiste and HEMELRYCK, Johannes Lodewyk Van. *Costumes belgiques, anciens et modernes.* Brussels, 1830.

MADOU, Jean Baptiste and EEKHOUT, J. J. *Collection des provinces de la Belgique.* Brussels, Burggraaf, 1835.

Luxemburg

DICKS, Edmond de la Fontaine. *Luxemburger Sitten und Bräuche.* Luxemburg, 1883.

HESS, Josef. *Luxemburger Volkskunde.* Luxemburg : Grevenmacher. London : Faber, 1929.

Germany

GENERAL WORKS

BAUR-HEINHOLD, Margarete. *Deutsche Trachten.* Königstein, Langewiesche, 1958.

DULLER, Eduard. *Das deutsche Volk.* Leipzig, Wigand, 1847.

HELM, Rudolf. *Deutsche Volkstrachten aus der Sammlung des Germanischen Museums in Nürnberg.* Munich, Lehmann, 1932.

HELM, Rudolf. *Die Bauerlichen Männertrachten im Germanischen Nationalmuseum zu Nürnberg.* Heidelberg, Winter, 1932.

HOTTENROTH, Friedrich. *Deutsche Volkstrachten.* 3 vols. Frankfurt, Keller, 1898–1902.

JULIEN, Rose. *Die Deutschen Volkstrachten.* Munich, Bruckmann, 1912.

KRETSCHMER, Albert. *Deutsche Volkstrachten.* Leipzig, Bach, 2nd. ed. 1887–90.

MUSÉE COSMOPOLITE. *Allemagne et Autriche.* Paris, 1850–63.

RETZLAFF, Hans. *Deutsche Bauerntrachten.* Berlin, Atlantis, 1934.

BADEN and WÜRTTEMBERG including THE BLACK FOREST

ADELMANN, Paula. *Das Mieder in der Volkstracht des Oberrheins.* Heidelberg, 1939.

BADER, Joseph. *Badische Volkssitten und Trachten.* Karlsruhe, Kunstverlag, 1843–44.

GLEICHAUF, Rudolf. *Badische Landestrachten im Auftrage des Grossherzog Badischen Handelsministeriums.* Stuttgart, Müller, 1862.

ISSEL, Heinrich, and JACOB, Hans. *Volkstrachten aus dem Schwarzwald.* Freiburg, Elchlepp, [1890].

LALLEMAND, Charles. *Les Paysans badois.* Strasbourg, Salomon, 1860.

PETTIGREW, Dora W. *Peasant costume of the Black Forest.* London, Black, 1937.

REINHARDT, Albert. *Schwarzwälder Trachten.* Karlsruhe, Badenia, 1968.

SCHREIBER, Aloys. *Trachten, Volkfeste und characteristische Beschäftigungen in Grosherzogtum Baden.* Freiberg, 1825.

BAYERN–BAVARIA

DÜNNINGER, Josef. *Unterfränkische Trachten.* Peter Geist, 1852.

GIERL, Irmgard. *Miesbacher Trachtenbuch. Die Bavern Tracht zwischen Isar und Inn.* Weissenhorn, Konrad, 1971.

GIERL, Irmgard. *Pfaffenwinkler Trachtenbuch.* Weissenhorn, Konrad, 1971.

LIPOWSKY, Félix Joseph. *Sammlung Bayerischer nationalcostume.* Munich, Hermann und Barth, 1830.

RATTELMÜLLER, Paul Ernst. *Dirndl, Janker, Lederhosen.* Munich, Gräfer und Unzer, 1970.

SCHÄDLER, Karl. *Die Lederhose in Bayern und Tirol.* Innsbruck, Wagner, 1962.

WEITNAUER, Alfred. *Tracht und Gwand im Schwabenland.* Kempten, Verlag für Heimatpflege, 1957.

ZABORSKY-WAHLSTÄTTEN, Oskar. *Die Tracht in Bayerischen und Böhmerwald.* Munish, Callwey, n.d.

ZELL, F. *Bauern-Trachten aus dem bayerischen Hochland.* Munich, 1903.

RHINELAND and HESSEN

AU, Hans von der. *Odenwalder Tracht.* Darmstadt, Leske, 1952.

BECKER, Karl August. *Die Volkstrachten der Pfalz.* Kaiserslautern, 1952.

DEIBEL, Hans. *Die Volkstrachten des Schlitzerlandes.* Marburg, Elwert, 1967.

HELM, Rudolf. *Hessische Bauerntrachten.* Marburg, Elwert, 1949.

JUSTI, Ferdinand. *Hessische Trachtenbuch.* Marburg, Elwert, 1905.

LÜCKING. Wolf, and HAIN, Mathilde. *Hessen.* Berlin, Akademie, 1959.

WESTPHALIA and LOWER SAXONY– NIEDERSACHSEN

LÜCKING, Wolf, and BRINGEMEIER, Martha. *Schaumburg-Lippe.* Berlin, Akademie, 1958.

SPIES, Gerd *Braunschweiger Volksleben nach Bildern von Carl Schröder, (1802–1867).* Brunswick, Waisenhaus, 1967.

WILLIE, Louis. *Die Trachten des Harzlandes.* Braunlage, Bonewitz,

LAUSITZ–LUSATIA : SORBISCHE TRACHTEN–WENDISH COSTUME

LANGEMATZ, Rolf, and NEDO, Paul. *Sorbische Volkskunst.* Bautzen, Domowina, 1968.

LÜCKING, W. and NEDO, Paul. *Die Lausitz. Sorbische Trachten.* Berlin, Akademie, 1956.

MESCHGANG, Jan [or Meškank, J.]. *Sorbische Volkstrachten II: Die Tracht der katholischen Sorben.* Bautzen, Domowina, 1957.

NEDO, Paul. *Sorbische Volkstrachten.* Bautzen, Domowina, 1954.

NOWAK-NEUMANN, Martin. *Sorbische Volkstrachten IV: Die Tracht der niederlausitzer Sorben.* Bautzen, Domowina, 1965.

NOWAK-NEUMANN, Martin, and NEDO, Paul. *Sorbische Volkstrachten I: Die Tracht der Sorben um Schleife.* Bautzen, Domowina, 1954.

SCHNEIDER, Erich [or Krawc, E.]. *Sorbische Volkstrachten III: Die Tracht der Sorben um Hoyerswerda [Wojerec].* Bautzen, Domowina, 1959.

MECKLENBURG

LEOPOLDI, Hans Heinrich. *Mecklenburgische Volkstrachten, I: Bauerntrachten.* Leipzig, Hofmeister, 1957.

THURINGIA

GERBING, Luise. *Die Thüringer Trachten in Wort und Bild.* Berlin, Stubenrauch, 1936.

SCHLESWIG-HOLSTEIN

HOFFMANN, Anna. *Die Probsteier Volkstracht.* Heide in Holstein, Westholsteinische Verlagsanstalt Boyens and Co., 1938.

HOFFMAN, Anna. *Die Landestrachten von Nordfriesland.* Heide in Holstein, Westholsteinische Verlagsanstalt Boyens and Co., 1940.

HOFFMAN, Anna. *Die Tracht des Kirchspiels Ostenfeld.* Heide in Holstein, Westholsteinische Verlagsanstalt Boyens and Co., 1953.

HOFFMAN, Anna. *Die Volkstrachten in Dithmarschen.* Westholsteinische Verlagsanstalt Boyens and Co., 1962.

Austria

GENERAL WORKS
FOCHLER, Rudolf. *Trachten aus Österreich.* Wels and Munich, Welsermühl, 1965.
BURGENLAND
HARTER, Helga. *Burgenländische Trachtenmappe.* [1938–9].
MAYER, Hans. *Burgenländisches Trachtenbuch.* Eisenstadt, 1938.
KÄRNTEN–CARINTHIA
BERTOLD, Hedwig, and PESENDORFER, Getrud. *Kärntner Trachten.* 5 portfolios. Klagenfurt, Kärnter Landsmannschaft, 1951.
KOSCHIER, Franz. 'Lebendige Volkstracht. Die Tracht und ihre Erneuerung,' *Kärntner Heimatleben 4.* Klagenfurt: Landesmuseum, 1960.
MORO, Gotbert. 'Zur Geschichte der Trachtenerneuerung in Kärnten,' Kärnten,' *Kärntner Heimatleben 4.* Klagenfurt, Landesmuseum, 1960.
NIEDERÖSTERREICH–LOWER AUSTRIA
GRÜNN, Helene. *Volkstracht in Niederösterreich.* 2. Teil. Linz, Trauner, 1971.
HESS-HABERLANDT, Gertrud. *Frauentrachten aus Niederösterreich.* Vienna, N.ö. Heimatwerk, 1952–54.
SCHMIDT, Leopold. *Volkstracht in Niederösterreich.* 1. Teil. Linz, Trainer, 1969.
OBERÖSTERREICH–UPPER AUSTRIA
OBERÖSTERREICHER HEIMATVEREIN. *Die oberösterreichische Landestracht für Frauen.* Linz, 1935.
SALZBURG
LANDESVERBAND DER TRACHTENVEREINE SALZBURG. *Salzburger Landestrachten.* Salzburg, 1935.
STEIERMARK–STYRIA
GERAMB, Victor von. *Zeitgemässe Steirertrachten.* Graz, Styria, 1936.
KAISER, Eduard. *38 Steiermarks Nationaltrachten und Festanzüge,* [1820].
MAUTNER, Konrad, and GERAMB, Victor von. *Steirisches Trachtenbuch.* 2 vols. Graz, 1932–39.
Steirische Trachten. Graz, Steirisches Volksbildungswerk, 1959.
TYROL
[HAMMERSTEIN, Hans von]. *Trachten der Alpenländer.* Vienna, Reichner, 1937.
KIRCHEBNER, Alois. *Neueste Volkstrachten aus Tirol in 12 Blättern.* Innsbruck, Schöpf, n.d.
Les habitants de Tyrol. Vienna, Stockl, [1820].
PESENDORFER, Gertrud. *Lebendige Tracht in Tirol.* Innsbruck, Wagner, 1966.
PESENDORFER, Gertrud, and KARASEK, Gretel. *Neue deutsche Bauerntrachten.* Tirol. Munich, 1938.
RINGLER, Josef and KARASEK, Gretel. *Tiroler Trachten.* Innsbruck, etc., Tyrolia, 1961.
SCHÄDLER, Karl. *Die Lederhose in Bayern und Tirol.* Innsbruck, Wagner, 1962.
SCHEDLER, Johan Georg. *Nationaltrachten von Tirol und Vorarlberg.* Innsbruck, [1824].
VORARLBERG
ILG, Karl. *Landes- und Volkskunde, Geschichte, Wirtschaft und Kunst Vorarlbergs.* 4 vols. Innsbruck, Wagner, 1961–68.
SCHEDLER, Johann Georg. *Nationaltrachten von Tirol und Vorarlberg.* Innsbruck, [1824].

Switzerland

AERNI-VON ERLACH, Felicitas. *Schweizer Trachten—Costumes suisses—Costumi svizzeri—Swiss national costumes.* Geneva, Éditions Générales, 1970.
ARX-LÜTHY, Frieda von. *Die Solothurner Trachten.* Solothurn, 1950.
BAUD-BOVY, Daniel. *Peasant art in Switzerland.* London, Studio, 1924.
BROCKMANN-JEROSCH, H. *Schweizer Volksleben, Sitten, Bräuchen, Wohnstätten.* Zurich, H.B-J, 1929.
Choix de costumes suisses, dessinés par des artistes du pays. Paris, Osterwald, 1826.
HEIERLI, Julie. *Die Klettgauer oder Hallauertracht des Kantons Schaffhausen.* Archives suisses des arts populaires, 1915.
HEIERLI, Julie. *Schweizerische Trachtenfeste,* 1923.
HEIERLI, Julie. *Die Volkstrachten von Bern, Freiburg und Wallis.* Erlenbach-Zurich, Rentsch, 1928.
HEIERLI, Julie. *Die Volkstrachten von Zurich, Schaffhausen, Graubünden und Tessin.* Erlenbach-Zurich, Rentsch, 1930.
HEIERLI, Julie. *Der Volkstrachten der Mittel- und Westschweiz. Luzen, Zug, Aargau, Solothurn, Basel, Waadt, Neuenberg und Geuf.* Erlenbach-Zurich, Rentsche, 1932.
HEIERLI, Julie. *Die Volkstrachten der Innerschweiz.* Erlenbach-Zurich, Rentsch, n.d.
HEIERLI, Julie. *Die Volkstrachten der Ostschweiz, Thurgau, St. Gallen, Glarus, Appenzell.* Erlenbach-Zurich, Rentsch, n.d.
HISTORISCHES MUSEUM, BERN. *Die Schweizer Trachtenbildnisse des Malers Joseph Reinhart.* Bern, 1961.
KÖNIG, Franz Niklaus. *Nouvelle collection de costumes suisses.* Zurich, Fuesli, [1803].
KÖNIG, Franz Niklaus. *Collection de costumes suisses.* Berne, [1804].
KÖNIG, Franz Niklaus. *Collection complette de costumes et occupations suisses . . .* Berne, 1822–30.
LAUR, Ernst, VIAL, Marie, and SCHLUEP-GRUBER, Martha. *Kleiden und Wohnen in Bauernhaus.* Bern, Buchverlag Verbandsdruckerei AG, 1951.
LAUR, Ernst, and WIRTH, Kurt. *Schweitzer Trachten.* Zurich, Silva, 1954.
LORY, Gabriel, and MORITZ, F. W. *Costumes suisses . . . dessins d'après nature.* Neuchatel, Wolrath, 1824.
MATHIS, Burkard, and ANGEHRN, Siegward. *Um Kleid und Tracht.* Einsiedeln, 1954.
MUSÉE COSMOPOLITE. *Suisse et Tyrol.* Paris, 1850–63.
Souvenirs de la Suisse. Paris, Arnauld Devresse, n.d.
SCHMID, D. A. *Trachtenfibel. The costumes of old Switzerland after the originals of D. A. Schmid.* [1791–1861]. Munich, Bruckmann, 1937.
SCHWEIZERISCHE VERKEHRSZENTRALE. *Die Schweizer Frau.* Text by Agnes von Segesser. Zurich, 1958.
WITZIG, Louise. *Les costumes suisses.* Fed. Nationale des costumes suisses, 1954.
WITZIG, Louise, and EBERLÉ, Edwige. *Costumes suisses.* Lausanne, Payot, 1959.
WITZIG, Louise, and EBERLÉ, Hedwig. *Schweizer Trachten.* Bern, Hallwag, 1959.
WYSS, P. *Trachten des Kantons Bern.* Bernische Trachtenvereiningung, 1944.
YOSY, A. *Switzerland as now divided into nineteen cantons . . . with picturesque representations of the dress and manners of the Swiss.* London, Booth, Murray, 1815.

Italy

GENERAL WORKS
CALDERINI, Emma. *Il costume popolàre in Italia.* Milan, Sperling and Kupfer, 1946.
GALANTI, Bianca M. *Dances of Italy.* London, Parrish, 1950.
GÖRLICH, Giovanni Gualtiero (ed.). *Costumi populari italiani.* 3 vols. Milan, Görlich, 1951–58.
HOLME, C. *Peasant art in Italy.* London, Studio, 1913.
MUSÉE COSMOPOLITE. *Italie,* Paris, 1850–63.
PINELLI, Bartolomeo. *Raccolta di cinquanta costumi pittoreschi incisi all' acquaforte . . .* Rome, 1809.
PINELLI, Bartolomeo. *Nuova raccolta di cinquanta costumi pittoreschi . . .* Rome, Antoni e Pavion, 1816.
PINGRET, Edouard Henri Théophile. *Galérie royale de costumes. Les Italiens.* Paris, 1841–48.
GENOA
PITTALUGA, A. *Duché de Gênes.* Paris, [1826].
PIEDMONT
CANZIANI, Estella, and ROHDE, Eleanor. *Piedmont.* London, Chatto, 1913.
TUSCANY
PIERACCINI, Francesco. *Collection de costumes des diverses provinces du Grand Duché de Toscane.* Paris, [1826].
VENETIA and the CARNIC ALPS
D'ORLANDI, L., and PERUSINI, G. *Il costume populare Carnico.* Udine, Doretti, 1966.
PERUSINI, G. *Il costume populare Udinese.* Udine, Doretti, 1966.

THE APENNINES and ABRUZZI

CANZIANI, Estella. *Through the Apennines and the lands of the Abruzzi.* Cambridge: Heffer, 1928.

NAPLES

BOURCARD, Francesco di. *Usi e costumi di Napoli.* Naples, Nobile, 1853–58.

PINELLI, Bartolomeo. *Raccolta di 50 costumi di Napoli.* Rome, 1814.

SARDINIA

ARATA, Guilio Ulisse, and BIASI, Guiseppe. *Arte sardi.* Milan, Fratelli Treves, [1935].

CARTA RASPI, Raimondo. *Costumi sardi.* Cagliari, [1930].

COSTA, Enrico. *Album di costumi Sardi.* In 10 parts. Sassari, Dessi, 1898–1901.

PITTALUGA, A. *Royaume de Sardaigne: costumes.* Paris, Marino, n.d.

SICILY

BERNADIS, C. de. *Sicilian costumes.* [1815–20].

France

BIBLIOGRAPHY

GENNEP, Arnold Van. *Manuel de folklore français contemporain.* Paris, Picard, 1938 and 1943–53. 4 vols in 8 (vol. 4 is a detailed critical bibliography).

GENERAL WORKS

GALLOIS, Émile. *Provinces françaises. Costumes décoratifs.* Paris, 1936.

GAUTHIER, Joseph (ed.). *L'art populaire français: costumes paysans.* Paris, Massin, 1930.

KAUFFMANN, P. *Les mariages pittoresques. Receuil de coutumes régionales. Texte et dessins de P. Kauffmann. 1. Alsace, Lorraine et Vosges, Ardennes et Bourgogne.* Paris, 1935.

KEIM, Aline. *Les costumes du pays de France présentés par A. Keim.* Paris, Nilsson, 1929.

LEPAGE-MEDVEY, E. *French costumes; with a preface by André Varagnac.* Paris. Hyperion, 1939.

Les Français, peints par eux-mêmes. Provinces. 3 vols. Paris, Curmer, 1841.

MUSÉE COSMOPOLITE. *Costumes français.* Paris, 1850–63.

PEAKE, Richard Brinsley. *The characteristic costume of France.* 1819–22.

ALSACE

KAUFFMANN, P. *L'Alsace tradionaliste.* Strasbourg, 1931. Reprinted, Colmar, 1970.

LAUGEL, Anselme. *Trachten und Sitten in Elsass.* Strasbourg, Fischbach, 1902.

AUVERGNE

LAS CASES, Philippe de. *L'art rustique en France: Auvergne.* Paris, Albin-Michel. 1933.

ROSSEL, André, and VIDAL, Jean. *Decouverte du costume Auvergnat. Texte liminaire commentaire et répertoire de Pierre François Aleil.* Paris, Hier et Demain, 1974.

TALBOT. *Auvergne. Costume du Puy de Dôme,* illustrated by C. Bour and Bertrand. Clermont-Farrand, [1865].

BERRI

LAPAIRE, Hugues. *Le pays berrichon.* Paris, Blond, 1908.

BORDEAUX

GALARD, Gustave de, and GERAUD, S. E. *Recueil des divers costumes des habitants de Bordeaux.* Bordeaux, Lavigne, [1818–19].

BOURGOGNE–BURGUNDY

GROUPE SPELEO-ARCHEOLOGIQUE CHAROLLAIS. *Les costumes traditionnels du Charollais et du Brionnais.* Dijon, Masseboeuf, 1971.

JEANTON, Gabriel. *Le Mâconnais traditionaliste et populaire, vol. 1: Le peuple; le costume; l'habitation.* Mâcon, Protat, 1920.

JEANTON, Gabriel. *Costumes bressans et mâconnais.* Mâcon, Renaudier, 1937.

BRETAGNE–BRITTANY

AUBERT, Octave Louis. *Les costumes bretons, leur histoire—leur évolution.* St. Brieuc, Aubert, 1936.

BIGOT, Maurice. *Les coiffes bretonnes; cent modèles differents.* St. Brieuc, Aubert, 1928.

CHOLEAU, Jean. *Costumes et chants populaires de Haute Bretagne.* Vitré, Unvaniez-Arvor, 1953.

CRESTON, R-Y. *Les costumes des populations bretonnes.* 5 fascicules. Rennes, Les Nouvelles de Bretagne, 1953–59.

DARJON, A. *Costumes bretons dessinés d'après nature.* [1860].

DARJON, A. *Costumes de la Bretagne.* Paris, 1865.

HÉLIAS, Pierre. *Danses de Bretagne: photographies de Jos Le Doaré.* Chateaulin, Jos Le Doaré, 1965.

HÉLIAS, Pierre. *Coiffes de Bretagne: photographies de Jos Le Doaré.* Chateaulin, Jos Le Doaré, 1967.

HÉLIAS, Pierre. *Costumes de Bretagne: photographies de Jos Le Doaré.* Chateaulin, Jos Le Doaré, 1969.

LALAISSE, Hippolyte (illustrator). *Costumes et coiffes de Bretagne, cent phototypies d'après les compositions de Hippolyte Lalaisse.* Paris, Laurens, n.d.

NORMANDY

ARINAL, Sylvain. *Decouverte du costume normand, commentaire par Sylvain Arinal.* Paris, Hier et Demain, 1974.

LALAISSE, Hippolyte. *La Normandie illustrée, lithographies par Hippolyte Lalaisse.* 2 vols., Nantes, Charpentier, 1852–55.

MAURICE, C. *Costumes pittoresques.* Paris, E. Morier, [1859].

POITOU

BILY-BROSSARD, Jeanne. *Coiffes et costumes féminins du Poitou.* Niort, Soulisse-Martin, 1952.

GELLE, P., and ARNAUD. C. *Vues et costumes pittoresques du département des Deux-Sèvres.* Niort, Morisset, 1844.

PROVENCE, SAVOIE, DAPHINÉ

CANZIANI, Estella. *Costumes, traditions and songs of Savoy.* London, Chatto, 1911.

CHARLES-ROUX, Jules. *Souvenirs du passé: le costume en Provence.* 2 vols. Paris, Lemerre, 1907.

DELAYE, Edmond. *Les anciens costumes des Alpes du Dauphiné.* Lyon, Grange et Giraud, 1922.

FLANDREYSY, Jeanne de. *La femme provençale.* Marseille, Detaille, 1922.

THE PYRENEES, NAVARRE, BASQUE COUNTRY

ARIZMENDI AMIEL, Maria Elena de. *Vascos y trajes.* 2 vols. San Sebastián, 1977.

DARTIGUENAVE, Alfred. *Costumes des Pyrénées dessinés d'après nature.* Pau, Bassy, [1860].

HARDING, J. D. *The costumes of the French Pyrénées.* London, 1832.

LE BONDIDIER, L. *Les vieux costumes pyrénéens.* Pau, Garet-Haristoy, [1917].

PINGRET, Édouard. *Costumes des Pyrén(n)ées.* Paris, Gihaut, [1840].

VEYRIN, Philippe. *Les Basques de Laband, de Soule et de Basse Navarre.* Paris, Arthaud, 1947 and 1955.

Spain and Portugal

BRADFORD, William. *Sketches of the country, character and costume in Portugal and Spain, 1808–1809.* London, Booth, 1810.

GALLOIS, Émile. *Le Costume en Espagne et au Portugal.* Paris, Laurens, 1954.

MUSÉE COSMOPOLITE. *Espagne et Portugal.* Paris, 1850–63.

Spain

GENERAL WORKS

AGUILERA, E. M. *Los trajes populares de España.* Barcelona, Omega, 1948.

ANDERSON, Ruth M. *Costumes painted by Sorolla in his 'Provinces of Spain'.* New York, Hispanic Society of America, 1951.

CARRERAS Y CANDI, F. *Folklore y costumbres de España.* 2 vols. Barcelona, 1931.

CRUZ CANO Y OLMEDILLA, Juan de la. *Colleccion de trajes de España, tanto antiguos como modernos.* Madrid, 1777.

Delineations of the most remarkable costumes of the different provinces of Spain. London, Stokes, 1822.

D'IVORI, Juan. *Vestidos tipicos de España.* Barcelona, Oribs, n.d.

GALLOIS, Émile. *Costumes espagnols.* Paris, Laurens, 1939.

GOMEZ TABANERA, Jose Manuel. *Trajes populares y costumbres tradicionales.* Madrid, Tesoro, 1950.

HOYOS SANCHOS, Nieves. *El traje regional en España*. Madrid, Ministry of Tourism, 1955.

ORTIZ ECHAGÜE, Jose. *España; tipos y trajes*. Madrid, Mayfe, 12th ed. 1971.

PALENCIA, Isabel de. *El traje regional de España*. Madrid, Voluntad 1926.

THE BALEARICS

CRUZ CANO Y OLMEDILLA, J. de la. *El traje Balear en doce láminas del siglo XVIII*. Palma, 1951.

CATALONIA

AMADES, Juan. *Indumentaria tradicional catalana*. Barcelona, La Neotipia, 1939.

EXTRAMADURA

ANDERSON, Ruth M. *Spanish costume; Extramadura*. New York, Hispanic Society, 1951.

HISPANIC SOCIETY OF AMERICA. *Extramadura costume: women's festival dress at Montehermoso, Caceres*. New York, H. Society, [1931].

GALICIA

ANDERSON, Ruth M. *The Gallegan provinces: Pontevedra and La Coruña*. New York, Hispanic Society, 1939.

HOYOS SANCHO, Nieves. *El traje regional de Galicia*. Santiago, 1971.

SALAMANCA

GARCIA BOIZA, Antonio. *El traje regional Salmantino*. Madrid, Espasa-Calpe, 1940.

HISPANIC SOCIETY OF AMERICA. *Choricero costume; Candelario, Salamanca*. From photographs in the collection of the Society. New York, 1931.

HISPANIC SOCIETY OF AMERICA. *Women's coiffure; Candelario, Salamanca*. New York, 1931.

HISPANIC SOCIETY OF AMERICA. *Women's dress for church; Candelario, Salamanca*. New York, 1931.

HISPANIC SOCIETY OF AMERICA. *Women's jewelry; Candelario, Salamanca*. New York, 1931.

HISPANIC SOCIETY OF AMERICA. *Costume of Candelario, Salamanca*. New York, 1932.

ARAGON AND THE PYRENEES

ARCO, Ricardo del. *El traje popular altoaragones*. Huesca, 1924.

ARCO, Ricardo del. *Costumbres y trajes en los Pirineos*. Saragossa, 1930.

VALENCIA

ALMELA VIVES, Francisco. *Historia del vestido de Labradora Valenciana*. Valencia Attración, 1962.

Portugal

ARMSTRONG, Lucille. *Dances of Portugal*. London, Parish, 1948.

ATHAYDE, Alfredo. 'Trajo', *A arte popular em Portugal*, 3. N.d.

BASTO, Cláudio. *Traje à Vianèsa*. Gaia, 1933.

CHAVES, Luis. 'O trajar do povo,' *Vida e arte do povo Portugês*. Oporto, 1940.

Costumes portuguezes, ou Colleçáo dos trajos, uzos, costumes mais motaveis e caracteristicos dos habitantes di Lisbo e provincias de Portugal. Lisbon, 1832.

LEVEQUE. *Costume of Portugal . . . illustrated by fifty coloured engravings with a description of the manners and usage of the country*. London, Colnaghi, 1814.

MACPHAIL. *Portuguese costumes*. Lisbon, Costa, [1841–42].

SOUZA, Alberto. *O trajo popular em Portugal nos seculos XVIII e XIX*.